I was excited to hear that Cheryl was writing a devotional called *Miracles of Jesus*. For the believer, Jesus' miracles are a constant reminder of His supreme power while foreshadowing the greatest of His miracles—His death and resurrection. Cheryl does a terrific job guiding the reader on this journey into Jesus' life and lordship, illustrating the importance of Jesus' miracles and their significance to the gospel. Jesus' acts of miracles serve as a road map to His ministry. Mark 1:15 tells us that Jesus performed many *miracles*, demonstrating His power over nature and spirits, and thus confirming that the Kingdom of God is at hand. Let Cheryl's insight and passion for Jesus guide you to discovering Christ's compassion for humanity. It is my prayer that this devotional will provide rich insight and bring comfort to your soul!

—JUDD BRANNON, director of the film *Champion*

C. K. SHARPE

MIRACLES OF JESUS

A 40-DAY DEVOTIONAL

BroadStreet
PUBLISHING

BroadStreet Publishing Group, LLC
Racine, Wisconsin, USA
BroadStreetPublishing.com

MIRACLES OF JESUS: A 40-DAY DEVOTIONAL

ISBN-13: 978-1-4245-5382-2 (softcover)
ISBN-13: 978-1-4245-5383-9 (e-book)

Stock or custom editions of BroadStreet Publishing titles may be purchased in bulk for educational, business, ministry, fundraising, or sales promotional use. For information, please e-mail info@broadstreetpublishing.com.

Cover design by Chris Garborg at www.garborgdesign.com
Typesetting by Katherine Lloyd at www.theDESKonline.com

Printed in the United States of America

17 18 19 20 21 5 4 3 2 1

Contents

FOREWORD

Devotional books strengthen authentic faith when they center the reader's thoughts upon Jesus Christ and root the reader's heart in God's Word. I am thankful to God that Cheryl Sharpe has provided the church one of those! Too often modern devotionals offer contemplative thoughts from the author and lose the gospel at the core. God's gospel is too great for us to set our hearts upon any person's mystical musings to start our day. Joyfully, this book sets the very words of God in front of us at the beginning of each chapter.

This devotional uniquely asks the reader to meditate on one of Jesus' miracles each day. These miracles unveil the majesty and sovereign power of our Lord and Savior. We gain a glimpse of the glory of God in the face of Jesus as we consider His miraculous works when He walked the earth. In a short space, we are given opportunity to meditate upon the content of each miracle, consider practical applications from each miracle, pray the message of the miracle into our lives, and finally jot down a few thoughts or prayers of our own. Each daily reading readies our soul to start our day communing with the living God who loves us and gave His Son for us.

I pray this book will be used to draw you deeper into the worship of our great Triune God.

—*Dr. Ritch Boerckel*, senior pastor,
Bethany Baptist Church near Peoria, Illinois

INTRODUCTION

Miracles either happened or they did not. What was the common denominator that prompted Jesus to perform the miracles that He did? Was it for personal gain? Recognition? Perhaps because He loved people so much? That's what I wanted to find out. Answering those questions became my heart's desire—my quest.

So I set out on my quest to study Jesus' New Testament miracles. I couldn't find anywhere in the Bible where Jesus performed a miracle for personal gain. His miracles were motivated by worthy intentions. They were instantaneous, they were done in front of witnesses, and they were always done in love—a feeling of compassion or concern by Jesus was apparent in each of His miracles.

I respect how Jesus interacted with people, revealing their measure of faith, forgiving their sin; and in an instant, drastically changing their purpose in life by placing them on the path of righteousness. I found He always demonstrated His unconditional love for humanity; an attribute He wants us to share as willingly as He does.

I invite you to read the truths that were revealed to me as I journeyed on my quest. Welcome to *Miracles of Jesus*, a forty-day devotional that strives to reveal the deep love Jesus had for people as He walked among us.

As you read the daily Scripture passages, may your heart fill with His love as you experience the richness of His works.

In the "Going Deeper" section, it is my desire that you glean insightful truths about our Lord Jesus.

"Personal Reflection" is your chance to reflect back on your life choices. As your heart prompts, please take the time to journal. A question has been posed to help get you started.

A "Prayer" and "Today's Truth" is included as a starting point for your worship time with God.

By reading the occasional poems, it is my hope you capture an inspired glimpse into these miraculous events.

May your mind crave more personal time with our Savior as you delve into His Word. May God continue to encourage and bless you on your journey with Him. I pray this devotional will encourage you in your daily walk with the Lord. The miracles of our Lord and Savior have touched the very core of my faith, and it is with pleasure that I share my heart with you.

—C. K. Sharpe

PART I

THE VIRGIN BIRTH

DAY 1

The Birth of Jesus the Messiah
The Miracle of God's Presence with Us

MATTHEW 1:18–25 NLT

This is how Jesus the Messiah was born. His mother, Mary, was engaged to be married to Joseph. But before the marriage took place, while she was still a virgin, she became pregnant through the power of the Holy Spirit. Joseph, to whom she was engaged, was a righteous man and did not want to disgrace her publicly, so he decided to break the engagement quietly.

As he considered this, an angel of the Lord appeared to him in a dream. "Joseph, son of David," the angel said, "do not be afraid to take Mary as your wife. For the child within her was conceived by the Holy Spirit. And she will have a son, and you are to name him Jesus, for he will save his people from their sins."

All of this occurred to fulfill the Lord's message through his prophet:

"Look! The virgin will conceive a child!
　She will give birth to a son,
and they will call him Immanuel,
　which means 'God is with us.'"

When Joseph woke up, he did as the angel of the Lord commanded and took Mary as his wife. But he did not have sexual relations with her until her son was born. And Joseph named him Jesus.

GOING DEEPER

The world would never be the same after Jesus' birth. God had come to earth in human form, not with a crown on His head, but humbly as a baby named Jesus. Every attribute, every point of character was that of God. His virgin mother brought to term the King that her nation had been promised for hundreds of years. He was wrapped in humble cloths and laid in a manger.

Salvation had come manifested in the birth of this God-child. Proof of this was made clear to the eye and mind on that starlit night in Bethlehem of Judea.

A humble few were given the good news and went to see the birth of the Messiah that night. How great the curiosity of the shepherds must have been; and perhaps, their eternal need for a Savior prompted them to see for themselves this "good news of great joy." A new King had been born.

Just as the shepherds sought out and paid homage to the newborn King of the Jews, Jesus seeks us today. Just as so many wise men and women sought and found Him so long ago, you too can seek and find Him today.

PERSONAL REFLECTION

Imagine looking down into the manger at little baby Jesus, knowing that lying there in that crude resting place was a child that would someday turn the world upside down.

What internal tug causes your heart to seek out Jesus today? Perhaps there is a longing built inside your soul that cries out for a Savior—the Messiah, the Lord—and draws you to that Godchild born so long ago. May your heart cry out with praise as you reflect on a baby born with the "soul purpose" of becoming a God-man—the One destined to be the Savior of the World.

In what area of your life do you need saving today?

PRAYER

Father, I approach your throne right now in awe of your great generosity. There are no words adequate to express the appreciation I have as I think about the life-changing birth that happened so long ago. Your love is limitless. You proved it to a world in need of a Savior by sending your Son as a newborn baby.

I give you all my praise for the birth of King Jesus and your great plan of salvation. Thank you for sending us the Redeemer of sins, and the hope of our rebirth in you. In Jesus' name I pray, amen.

TODAY'S TRUTH

JESUS IS FULLY
GOD AND
FULLY HUMAN.

PART II

CONTROL OF NATURE

Jesus Turns Water into Wine
The Miracle of Faith

JOHN 2:1–11 NLT

The next day there was a wedding celebration in the village of Cana in Galilee. Jesus' mother was there, and Jesus and his disciples were also invited to the celebration. The wine supply ran out during the festivities, so Jesus' mother told him, "They have no more wine."

"Dear woman, that's not our problem," Jesus replied. "My time has not yet come."

But his mother told the servants, "Do whatever he tells you."

Standing nearby were six stone water jars, used for Jewish ceremonial washing. Each could hold twenty to thirty gallons. Jesus told the servants, "Fill the jars with water." When the jars had been filled, he said, "Now dip some out, and take it to the master of ceremonies." So the servants followed his instructions.

When the master of ceremonies tasted the water that was now wine, not knowing where it had come from (though, of course, the servants knew), he called the bridegroom over. "A host always serves the best wine first," he said. "Then, when everyone has had a lot to drink, he brings out the less expensive wine. But you have kept the best until now!"

This miraculous sign at Cana in Galilee was the first time Jesus revealed his glory. And his disciples believed in him.

GOING DEEPER

The wine was to last throughout the weeklong wedding feast, but the beverage ran out. There were many distinguished guests and teachers in attendance, and the bride and groom would suffer disgrace and embarrassment from this social blunder. A woman pointed to a man and told the servants to obey whatever He asked of them.

They went to that man and then did as He requested. Later, they would hear more about this man named Jesus. They would probably never forget the day they had filled the pots with water and watched as the water was transformed into wine; the best wine served at the celebration.

Jesus' disciples would not forget that day either, but for an entirely different reason. This day was the first time they witnessed Jesus' divine nature. As His power was revealed to them, the disciples placed their faith in Him.

Jesus' desire continues today to turn weak faith into strong faith, just as He did with the disciples—one faith-building experience at a time.

PERSONAL REFLECTION

In what circumstances have you found yourself in a position of not knowing where to go for help in a difficult situation? You know that God is your provider, but did you realize He is the source, He is the point of origin, and He is always ready to give His best to you? Have faith; dear one, He is willing to meet your needs.

So do as Jesus' mother did. Hurriedly and with unwavering expectations run straight to the source of power for help.

God will take your seemingly impossible problems and resolve them if you only ask. Prayer is your direct line of communication to a loving God—a God that can work a miracle in your life. Dear one, let not your faith be found lacking. Jesus always gives His best. He is the provider of *all* your needs: spiritually, emotionally, physically, and materially.

Hear Him saying, "Ask! I want you to ask!" If you would like to see God work in your life more often, ask more often.

With what faith-filled experience has God blessed you?

PRAYER

Father, thank you for always giving your best. I desire to give you my best, my full energy. I ask that you increase my belief one faith-building experience at a time as Jesus did with His disciples. Through your power, may I help advance your Kingdom with the amount of faith I have now. Please give me your grace as I serve you. Thank you for providing wise counsel according to your Word through bringing the right people, at the right time, into my life. Indeed, my cup runs over knowing you are my ever-present God. In Jesus' name I pray, amen.

TODAY'S TRUTH

JESUS IS A
FAITH BUILDER.

First Miraculous Catch of Fish

The Miracle of Trusting Jesus

LUKE 5:1–11 NLT

One day as Jesus was preaching on the shore of the Sea of Galilee, great crowds pressed in on him to listen to the word of God. He noticed two empty boats at the water's edge, for the fishermen had left them and were washing their nets. Stepping into one of the boats, Jesus asked Simon, its owner, to push it out into the water. So he sat in the boat and taught the crowds from there.

When he had finished speaking, he said to Simon, "Now go out where it is deeper, and let down your nets to catch some fish."

"Master," Simon replied, "we worked hard all last night and didn't catch a thing. But if you say so, I'll let the nets down again." And this time their nets were so full of fish they began to tear! A shout for help brought their partners in the other boat, and soon both boats were filled with fish and on the verge of sinking.

When Simon Peter realized what had happened, he fell to his knees before Jesus and said, "Oh, Lord, please leave me— I'm such a sinful man." For he was awestruck by the number of fish they had caught, as were the others with him. His partners, James and John, the sons of Zebedee, were also amazed.

Jesus replied to Simon, "Don't be afraid! From now on you'll be fishing for people!" And as soon as they landed, they left everything and followed Jesus.

GOING DEEPER

Not everyone has a boat that Jesus can get in, but everyone has a heart in which He can reside. And, after we have asked Him in, He will take us places and give us opportunities that we would never have imagined. Jesus says, "Give me your heart. May your eyes take delight in following My ways."

The disciples, although somewhat skeptical at first, took Jesus at His word when He told them to go out into the deep to catch some fish. They trusted that He was telling them where to navigate to a great fishing spot.

Jesus was interested in their lives, and He is interested in ours too. Let us not be skeptical. When He directs our life, following Him in obedience as the disciples did, results in living out our calling as Christ-followers in a fallen world. Jesus knows where we need to go each day. We need to trust Him as He points us in the right direction.

The Scriptures encourage us in Proverbs 3:5–6 to "Seek his will in all you do, and he will show you which path to take" (NLT). Look to His Word. It is always a good place to start. We can hear God's heart and voice through His words. All we need to do is listen, trust, and follow His leadership.

PERSONAL REFLECTION

What a rewarding and personal experience to know Jesus will be with you as you go about your day's journey. You only have to trust Him. Take a moment to picture in your mind handing Jesus your cares as you get up each morning. There is a myriad of possibilities for which you can worry; your to-do list, your children, your spouse, your job, your income, or how to make better use of your time. Just remember this; the disciples' skepticism changed to trust as they hauled in a net full of fish.

Today you can trust His instruction as you listen to God's voice. Your catch will be big also, but might not come in the form of fish. Listen to Jesus and know His instructions will yield a great catch. You can trust and depend on the Lord. Move from worry to worship and give Jesus your day.

In what ways are you going to trust Jesus with your day?

PRAYER

Dear Jesus, I gladly give you my net to fill according to your will so that I may be supplied by your hand alone and not my own. Whether my net is seemingly empty or when it is full of uncountable blessings, I thank you for your provision. I trust you to meet my needs.

My heart overflows with gratefulness as I partake daily of your loving-kindness. I am thankful for the presence of you in my life. I praise you for who you are. My life has been immeasureably blessed since I decided to follow you. Thank you, Jesus. Amen.

TODAY'S TRUTH

TRUST JESUS, FOR
HE WILL GUIDE YOU.

Jesus Calms the Storm

The Miracle of Jesus' Calming Spirit

LUKE 8:22–25 NLT

One day Jesus said to his disciples, "Let's cross to the other side of the lake." So they got into a boat and started out. As they sailed across, Jesus settled down for a nap. But soon a fierce storm came down on the lake. The boat was filling with water, and they were in real danger.

The disciples went and woke him up, shouting, "Master, Master, we're going to drown!"

When Jesus woke up, he rebuked the wind and the raging waves. Suddenly the storm stopped and all was calm. Then he asked them, "Where is your faith?"

The disciples were terrified and amazed. "Who is this man?" they asked each other. "When he gives a command, even the wind and waves obey him!"

GOING DEEPER

Imagine yourself in a small, open fishing boat with Jesus and His disciples out in the middle of the beautiful Sea of Galilee.

Several of Jesus' followers had been simple fishermen before Jesus made them fishers of men. They knew the intensity of the northerly winds plummeting down the upper Jordan Valley and the deadly potential of the winds meeting the warmer air over the Galilee Basin. A calm and pleasant day could turn into a raging storm.

It would be easy for fear to take hold as an unexpected storm poured water into the boat wave after wave. Psalm 89:8–9 declares these words about God, "Who is like you, LORD God Almighty? You, LORD, are mighty, and your faithfulness surrounds you. You rule over the surging sea; when its waves mount up, you still them" (NIV).

When Jesus rebuked the storm, whether or not the disciples realized it, they had been taken to another level of understanding the faithfulness of their Lord. They were learning to trust His word. It is the same for us today. His faithfulness reassures us of His desire to take care of us. Our faith grows in the midst of our storms because of His presence. There is no danger, hardship, or fear that He can't take you through.

PERSONAL REFLECTION

When we are going through a storm in our life, there is no sailing around it. Since Jesus saved the disciples from a raging storm, we can expect He is more than able to rescue us, His redeemed ones, from storms of sickness, loss of jobs or loved ones, marriage issues, or whatever storm is in our path today. Call out to Him and have faith in His power. He brought calm to the disciples, and He can bring calm to our spirit.

In the midst of storms, we should lift our voices to Him in prayer and thank Him for being our Savior. Let it be our testimony.

*When has Jesus proved His faithfulness
to you during a turbulent time?*

PRAYER

*Oh Lord, thank you for your faithfulness. You display your
mighty works through the power of your hands. Jesus, I trust
you as threats of turmoil rise in my life and threaten to sink me
into murky water, that you will lift me to safety. Let me cling
to you in faith and trust in your unwavering love.*

*With peace in my heart, I slumber under your protection.
May I never doubt you, but rest in the assurance that you are
in control of my life. May my faith in you be sufficient, so
I might remain calm in times of raging waters. Thank you,
Jesus, for your listening ear and supportive care. Amen.*

TODAY'S TRUTH

JESUS IS FAITHFUL.

Lord of the Storm

By C. K. Sharpe

Silence the roaring of the waves
Faith of your believer wavers
I cry out in time of trouble
Lord of the Storm.

Your vessel rocks as my faith stumbles
Oh, One with power over tempest
Bring silence to life's roaring waves
Lord of the Storm.

God grant me calm to my tumult
May I rest in faith midst waves throws
Conquer doubt so my heart knows
Lord of the Storm.

Jesus Feeds
the Five Thousand

The Miracle of Abundance

LUKE 9:10–17 NLT

When the apostles returned, they told Jesus everything they had done. Then he slipped quietly away with them toward the town of Bethsaida. But the crowds found out where he was going, and they followed him. He welcomed them and taught them about the Kingdom of God, and he healed those who were sick.

Late in the afternoon the twelve disciples came to him and said, "Send the crowds away to the nearby villages and farms, so they can find food and lodging for the night. There is nothing to eat here in this remote place."

But Jesus said, "You feed them."

"But we have only five loaves of bread and two fish," they answered. "Or are you expecting us to go and buy enough food for this whole crowd?" For there were about 5,000 men there.

Jesus replied, "Tell them to sit down in groups of about fifty each." So the people all sat down. Jesus took the five loaves and two fish, looked up toward heaven, and blessed them. Then, breaking the loaves into pieces, he kept giving the bread and fish to the disciples so they could distribute it to the people.

They all ate as much as they wanted, and afterward, the disciples picked up twelve baskets of leftovers!

GOING DEEPER

There may be times in life when we are called on to "split our last beans." Looking at those few beans one might say to the Lord, "But Lord, there aren't enough beans." Trust in His succificiency, the great multiplier of provisions.

One way God meets the needs of His people is through others. When God calls us to be the vessels of provision, do not hesitate to share. The Kingdom of heaven works through us at our workplace, homes, and in the community. With joy in our hearts, be a basket-bearer for Him, grateful to the One that provides for all needs.

Because Jesus has great compassion for people and He is aware of the power of God, He told the disciples to feed the people. In the same way, as we feel the power of God in our life and are called to serve others, we gladly do it.

As our hearts fill with the joy of the Lord in doing His requests, may we find blessing others is more satisfying than the gift we shared. Lift your head up to the Lord and ask Him to make you a blessing to someone today.

PERSONAL REFLECTION

Every day you are given abundant grace and mercy to live out the life God has planned just for you. You have been abundantly blessed in many ways; by means that are especially for you. God blesses us with a set amount of time, talent, and resources. You probably will not be called upon to feed the multitudes as the disciples were, but you can do your best to be a blessing to those God directs you to in your life.

As you appreciate and enjoy the blessings you have been given from God, you will find it is a joy to bless others with your fruit. What a joy it is to serve the Lord in this way.

As you thank Him for His acts of daily provision for your home, life, and family, be sure to thank Him for His abundant love and the indwelling of the Holy Spirit in your life. You serve a God that provides abundantly.

In what ways have you been abundantly blessed by God?

PRAYER

Dear Jesus, my heart sings with the knowledge that you are the God of abundance. As I take inventory of my storehouse, please make me aware of the needs of others in my neighborhood, community, area schools, and churches. Prompt me to be a basket-bearer, willing to share, willing to help others.

As you said in Matthew, "Truly, I say to you, as you did it to one of the least of these of my brothers, you did it to me." Oh Lord, may your will be done through me. I am thankful, God, that you are all knowing and provide for those in need through your love and your loved ones. In Jesus' name, amen.

TODAY'S TRUTH

GOD BLESSES ABUNDANTLY.

Jesus Walks on Water

The Miracle of Authority Over Nature

MATTHEW 14:22–33 NLT

Immediately after this, Jesus insisted that his disciples get back into the boat and cross to the other side of the lake, while he sent the people home. After sending them home, he went up into the hills by himself to pray. Night fell while he was there alone.

Meanwhile, the disciples were in trouble far away from land, for a strong wind had risen, and they were fighting heavy waves. About three o'clock in the morning Jesus came toward them, walking on the water. When the disciples saw him walking on the water, they were terrified. In their fear, they cried out, "It's a ghost!"

But Jesus spoke to them at once. "Don't be afraid," he said. "Take courage. I am here!"

Then Peter called to him, "Lord, if it's really you, tell me to come to you, walking on the water."

"Yes, come," Jesus said.

So Peter went over the side of the boat and walked on the water toward Jesus. But when he saw the strong wind and the waves, he was terrified and began to sink. "Save me, Lord!" he shouted.

Jesus immediately reached out and grabbed him. "You have so little faith," Jesus said. "Why did you doubt me?"

When they climbed back into the boat, the wind stopped. Then the disciples worshiped him. "You really are the Son of God!" they exclaimed.

GOING DEEPER

Picture the colder mountain air rushing down the Jordan Rift Valley causing a horrific thunderstorm on the Sea of Galilee. The disciples were right in the middle of one of those storms. Most of the men were seasoned fishermen and well acquainted with the local weather, but still, it took great strength to keep their boat from sinking. The violent winds and raging waves had been going on for hours. Would it never stop? The shoreline had long since disappeared. There seemed no end to the disciples' battle with nature.

Jesus came to them. He came to them during the fourth watch—around three a.m.—*walking* on the water. They did not recognize their Master at first because they did not expect Him in these circumstances. Because of Jesus' authority, the winds and waves abated. The sea calmed.

Watching Jesus walking on water that morning through a vicious storm, revealed Jesus authority over nature and His divinity as well. For the first time since the disciples were called, they realized and acknowledged in faith that this man Jesus, who just walked on water, was God.

PERSONAL REFLECTION

Jesus will walk on water for us. He extends His saving hand out to us when we feel life's waters are overwhelming us. Whether these storms come in the form of trials, stress, temptations, illnesses, or grief over loss, we don't have to feel afraid or be alone.

Though it may be difficult at times, we need to cling to our faith—God is with us just the same as He was with His disciples. All we have to do is reach out, take His hand, and let Him lift us from life's rising waters.

Go to the Lord in prayer over your concerns. Any trial can make you start to doubt, but it is precisely during those times that God wants to take you out of your storm and wrap you in His comforting and protective care.

What does Jesus' walking on water look like for you today?

PRAYER

Dear Lord, you are my strength and my salvation. Through your Scriptures, I am assured that you are walking in my storms right beside me. I trust in your promise that you will never leave me nor forsake me. I have faith in you and all that you are and do. You are a very present help in times of trouble. I place myself solely in your care, knowing you bring peace to life's waves of demand.

I am so glad that you want me to call out to you whenever I experience physical, emotional, or spiritual storms. I gladly take your hand. You are my Comforter during storms and the Son that shines in my heart. Amen.

TODAY'S TRUTH

JESUS COMES TO US WALKING ON THE WATER IN OUR STORMS.

Miraculous Feeding of the 4,000
The Miracle of Compassion

MATTHEW 15:32–39 NLT

Then Jesus called his disciples and told them, "I feel sorry for these people. They have been here with me for three days, and they have nothing left to eat. I don't want to send them away hungry, or they will faint along the way."

The disciples replied, "Where would we get enough food here in the wilderness for such a huge crowd?"

Jesus asked, "How much bread do you have?"

They replied, "Seven loaves, and a few small fish."

So Jesus told all the people to sit down on the ground. Then he took the seven loaves and the fish, thanked God for them, and broke them into pieces. He gave them to the disciples, who distributed the food to the crowd.

They all ate as much as they wanted. Afterward, the disciples picked up seven large baskets of leftover food. There were 4,000 men who were fed that day, in addition to all the women and children. Then Jesus sent the people home, and he got into a boat and crossed over to the region of Magadan.

GOING DEEPER

Jesus had been talking to the crowds for several days on a mountain near the Sea of Galilee. The people had been sitting and listening intently. They had never heard Scripture explained the way that He was teaching it. This spiritual man, this Jesus they were looking to, spoke as one having authority. He had a kindness and truth in His voice that captured their attention, and they couldn't wait to hear more. He spoke about spiritual matters and the way to live more abundantly. With each word He spoke, one would think He was talking personally to them instead of to a crowd

For many, it was a life-changing event, possibly an experience that would cause them to examine their life and change how they were living it.

Jesus had completed His time of teaching and healing of the people. He was filled with compassion as He saw their exhausted food supply and weary faces. Jesus was not willing to send them home without sustenance. He cared about their physical as well as their spiritual needs.

Jesus directed the disciples to find food for the crowds. Why did He do that? Jesus delighted in meeting the needs of others, and He probably wanted the disciples to experience the same enjoyment. The disciples gathered what food there was and God blessed it abundantly.

What fullness we can have in our soul knowing Jesus meets our needs. In turn, we can be used for His glory to compassionately and kindly meet the needs of others.

PERSONAL REFLECTION

Jesus is your compassionate and kind Lord. He cares deeply about everything that concerns you. Just as Jesus petitioned God for His blessing upon the seven loaves and a few small fish, you too can take your requests to God in prayer. No matter how small you think your petition, He is faithful to meet your need abundantly. He is the great multiplier. Jesus guarantees us in Scripture that He is the Bread of Life and whoever comes to Him shall not hunger. He goes on to say that whoever believes in Him shall never thirst. His kindness knows no limits for Jesus Christ is the same yesterday, and today, and tomorrow. You can count on it. He indeed is the Bread of Life; eternally and here on earth.

What need do you have right now? Ask God to meet that need.

PRAYER

Lord, I think about the hope the people must have had as they sat and listened to you. Then to have the pleasure of sitting at your table as a guest while you gave them a meal.

It makes my heart overflow with thankfulness to know that you satisfy my deepest hungers—indeed provide me with the fullness of your Word, your Spirit in my soul, and more than sufficiently provide for the daily needs of my body. Thank you for the kindness and grace you show this undeserving person. I look forward to breaking bread with you someday, dear Lord. Amen.

TODAY'S TRUTH

JESUS COMPASSIONATELY PROVIDES OUR NEEDS.

Miraculous Temple Tax in a Fish's Mouth

The Miracle of Tax Delivery

MATTHEW 17:24–27 NLT

On their arrival in Capernaum, the collectors of the Temple tax came to Peter and asked him, "Doesn't your teacher pay the Temple tax?"

"Yes, he does," Peter replied. Then he went into the house.

But before he had a chance to speak, Jesus asked him, "What do you think, Peter? Do kings tax their own people or the people they have conquered?"

"They tax the people they have conquered," Peter replied.

"Well, then," Jesus said, "the citizens are free! However, we don't want to offend them, so go down to the lake and throw in a line. Open the mouth of the first fish you catch, and you will find a large silver coin. Take it and pay the tax for both of us."

GOING DEEPER

God initiated the first tax for the upkeep of the Tabernacle in the time of Moses. The amount paid had fluctuated throughout the years, but it was a tax the Jews expected to pay annually. Every male Jew, twenty years of age and up, now paid an annual half-shekel. Along with the Roman government's tremendous taxes, the Jewish community felt the yoke of burden upon their shoulders.

Even the collection containers along the provincial roadsides were a demanding reminder that taxes were due. In other words, this voluntary tax was expected to be paid.

Sons of kings were exempt from paying taxes. Wouldn't Jesus, the Son of the King of all creation, be excused from paying tax on a house that belonged to His Father? Of course, He should be.

Jesus used Peter's answer to the tax collector as a growth opportunity for Peter (and a lesson in humility). Jesus didn't want to offend the community by not paying the tax, so He sent Peter, this net fisherman, to the lake to go fishing with a hook and line. Peter's trip yielded the coin in the fish's mouth just as Jesus had said. Wonder what expression was on Peter's face as he opened the mouth of that fish and saw the coin. Nevertheless—lesson learned, problem solved, tax paid.

PERSONAL REFLECTION

It is not likely you will ever have tax money provided in the mouth of a fish. Today payroll deductions or personal savings help you to meet your tax bills when they come due.

Jesus often uses unexpected ways and resources to answer prayers of need. Perhaps it is the neighbor who knocks on the door with a much-appreciated food item, a telephone call with an offer of a ride to work, roadside help with a flat tire, or that card from Grandma with a few extra dollars in it. Through His unexpected provision, we learn that He loves to provide; sometimes in very unique ways.

---

*What unique way has God
provided in your time of need?*

PRAYER

God, I know you care about me, and you love to provide
for me. Help me to lean on your understanding. Let the way
you lived on earth be a daily reminder to me to apply your
examples of faith, prayer, and humility in every part of my
life. I think you are the kindest, most caring person who has
ever walked the earth.

I was blessed by reading the miracle of supplying tax money
in the mouth of a fish. By this miracle, you have shown me
that you are sufficient to meet all of my family's need through
your riches in glory. Thank you for daily provisions and witnessing your power in those times of unexpected provision.
Your love fails not. Thank you so much, Lord. Amen.

TODAY'S TRUTH

JESUS MEETS OUR NEEDS;
SOMETIMES IN
UNEXPECTED WAYS.

DAY 9

Jesus Curses the Fig Tree
The Miracle of God's Judgment

MARK 11:12–14 NLT

The next morning as they were leaving Bethany, Jesus was hungry. He noticed a fig tree in full leaf a little way off, so he went over to see if he could find any figs. But there were only leaves because it was too early in the season for fruit. Then Jesus said to the tree, "May no one ever eat your fruit again!" And the disciples heard him say it.

GOING DEEPER

The fig tree, located along the wayside, was commonly picked and eaten by travelers. This particular fig tree had lush foliage indicating fruit, but it did not have any. When we stand before the Lord, our spiritual branches will either be found bare or filled with fruit. It is up to each one of us to keep our branches nourished and fruit filled.

God gives us plenty of time to turn from our sin. He is long-suffering; however, when time runs out we are cut down. Let's be faithful to live a life consistent with our faith. Let's exercise our power of prayer and share our fruit. So one day, when we stand before our Creator, He will see in us the fruit of the Spirit that He expects to find.

Personal Reflection

How do we obtain the fruit of the Spirit? We can't buy it, fake it, or borrow it. We receive it through an outpouring of the Holy Spirit who resides in us. He has gifted us with one or more of the following fruit: love, joy, peace, patience, kindness, goodness, faithfulness, gentleness, and self-control.

As we grow in our faith, our desire to share our fruit will grow. We will want to use it for God's glory. We must ask the Holy Spirit to guide us so that we might see our fruit grow to full maturity and ripe for the sharing. In that way we can let our fruit become a living testament as to who we are in Christ.

Which fruit of the Spirit do you see sweet evidence of in your life? Which do you want to grow?

Prayer

Dear Father, I do not want to be like the fig tree with leaves promising fruit but failing to deliver any. Help me, through your power, to live a life of fruitfulness.

It is my prayer that when you look for my fruit, you will not be surprised to find sweet evidence of a genuine life lived in faith. In Jesus' precious name I pray, amen.

TODAY'S TRUTH

GOD JUDGES
ONE'S SPIRITUAL FRUIT.

Where Is the Fruit

By C. K. Sharpe

Wood twisted by age is tree's rightful heritage
Growing proudly by wayside for all to see
With limbs stretched out revealing impressive foliage.

Early on leaves promising figs prove barren
Magnificent lush leaves are all you can see;
But if there's no fruit, what value is the tree?

What of pious man, is he not like cursed tree
Pledging harvest of good for all men to see
As for spiritual fruit, he'll never bare any.

What of their fruit for there is none
Does not the Lord expect some?

The Miracle of His Provision

Second Miraculous Catch of Fish

JOHN 21:4–14 NLT

At dawn Jesus was standing on the beach, but the disciples couldn't see who he was. He called out, "Fellows, have you caught any fish?"

"No," they replied.

Then he said, "Throw out your net on the right-hand side of the boat, and you'll get some!" So they did, and they couldn't haul in the net because there were so many fish in it.

Then the disciple Jesus loved said to Peter, "It's the Lord!" When Simon Peter heard that it was the Lord, he put on his tunic (for he had stripped for work), jumped into the water, and headed to shore. The others stayed with the boat and pulled the loaded net to the shore, for they were only about a hundred yards from shore. When they got there, they found breakfast waiting for them—fish cooking over a charcoal fire, and some bread.

"Bring some of the fish you've just caught," Jesus said. So Simon Peter went aboard and dragged the net to the shore. There were 153 large fish, and yet the net hadn't torn.

"Now come and have some breakfast!" Jesus said. None of the disciples dared to ask him, "Who are you?" They knew it was the Lord. Then Jesus served them the bread and the fish. This was the third time Jesus had appeared to his disciples since he had been raised from the dead.

GOING DEEPER

In the dawn of the morning, Jesus called out to His disciples from the shore. This shoreline was the same shore from which Jesus first called four of His followers, promising to make them fishers of men. Many of the men had returned to their trade after Jesus' death. As they began recognizing who was calling them, Peter's excitement became so great that he jumped overboard and swam to shore to be with the Lord.

What a God of provision we have. When the others got to shore, they found Jesus sitting beside a charcoal fire with fish and bread. The Lord was making breakfast for them. He asked them to bring some of their catch, showing them that He and the disciples were working together to provide the nourishment they were about to enjoy. What could be more exciting than eating breakfast with the resurrected Jesus?

The preparation of fish and bread for His disciples was perhaps an unspoken analogy foretelling His disciples that their life of ministry was about to begin full time? They would have the privilege of *fishing* for men, women, and children and providing spiritual nourishment of the *Bread* of Life. What wonderful life-changing provisions this would be for the souls with whom they would soon come in contact.

Let's not forget that we too have been wonderfully made for His service. Go and shine in His glory.

PERSONAL REFLECTION

If you happened to see a friend entering a restaurant where you were eating, you would probably call out a greeting, and perhaps invite them to join you at your table. After sharing stories about what's been going on in your lives, you would tell each other about your plans for the future.

So it was with the Lord after His resurrection. He called out to His disciples from the shore to enjoy breakfast with Him after they had spent a long night of fishing. The disciples were enthusiastic as they talked about how working together they could spread the "good news" throughout the generations.

You are called, as are all Christians, to be fishers of men. You are privileged to take the good news and tell others about the love of the Lord. May He bless you as you spread the gospel throughout the generations.

In what ways are you being a fisher of men and spreading the gospel of Jesus Christ to others?

PRAYER

May I, as your child through Christ, call out to the unsaved and nourish them in the feast of your words. When they depart from the banquet table, may they have found fullness through your salvation message.

I am grateful for your heart that desires your children to become fishers of men. Bless all of your children, for these are your salt and light of the earth—a group that brings others to you through the faithful witness of what you completed at

Calvary. Please keep these, your fishers of men, strong and safe as they spread the good news throughout the generations until the great day of your return. Amen.

TODAY'S TRUTH

JESUS WANTS US TO TELL OF HIS HEART FOR OTHERS BY BEING FISHERS OF MEN:

PART III

DELIVERANCE

Jesus Drives Out an Impure Spirit
The Miracle of Jesus' Power Over Evil

LUKE 4:31–36 NIV

Then he went down to Capernaum, a town in Galilee, and on the Sabbath he taught the people. They were amazed at his teaching, because his words had authority.

In the synagogue there was a man possessed by a demon, an impure spirit. He cried out at the top of his voice, "Go away! What do you want with us, Jesus of Nazareth? Have you come to destroy us? I know who you are—the Holy One of God!"

"Be quiet!" Jesus said sternly. "Come out of him!" Then the demon threw the man down before them all and came out without injuring him.

All the people were amazed and said to each other, "What words these are! With authority and power he gives orders to impure spirits and they come out!"

GOING DEEPER

As usual, the townspeople were gathering for Sabbath in the synagogue. They were used to seeing Jesus behind the pulpit when He was in town, and this was one of those days. He always brought them a message of repentance and "good news" about the Kingdom of God. They didn't realize that not only had

God's word came down to earth, but also that God's authority and power had as well, and they were about to witness both.

A man, possessed by a demon, was also in attendance. The demon immediately recognized Jesus as God and feared Jesus. What the demon heard Jesus saying to the people was exactly the opposite of satan's goals. This chance encounter was not going to end well. And it didn't—for the demon.

The people were amazed at what their eyes saw, and their ears heard as Jesus called out the demon from this man. They heard Jesus speaking firmly and with great authority. Some who witnessed this miracle started believing that perhaps this was the Son of God after all. However, those that were hard-hearted didn't like it, not one little bit.

When the Lord's work is genuinely being done, satan will always oppose it. Our authority and power are in the Lord. He is with us. As His own remain strong in the Lord, even a little of His strength is sufficient. Living an obedient, faithful, and Spirit-empowered life is what enables us to stand firm.

PERSONAL REFLECTION

There was a potential of a whole room full of people to be set free by the truth of God's words. A demon intended to destroy God's time with the people.

When you sense a heart is ready to hear the message of salvation and God prompts you to witness to that person, you probably have had times when unforeseen situations yell out to disrupt the moment. When this happens to you, stand firm in the power of the Lord, and refuse to acquiesce to satan. Stand firm for Jesus is with you. He has always given you the power and authority to accomplish His work. Say a quick silent prayer, and go ahead and plant the seed that Jesus intended. He will take care of the soul harvest *and* the disrupter of the moment.

---

*What do you do to oppose a
disruption during a time of witnessing?*

PRAYER

Dear Father, thank you for seeing and hearing all that goes on in my life. Please give me boldness to stand firm against any opposition of the faith that comes against me. I know you have power over evil and will expel interruptions of wickedness. May the foundation of my faith never waver but be upheld through the reading of your Word and obedience to it. As you walk with me and I witness your truth, allow your strength to stand firm within me. I am anxious to tell of the great things you have done in my life and will do in others' lives. In His holy name, amen.

TODAY'S TRUTH

JESUS HAS AUTHORITY
OVER EVIL.

Jesus Heals Many Sick at Evening
The Miracle of Trusting Jesus

LUKE 4:40–41 NIV

At sunset, the people brought to Jesus all who had various kinds of sickness, and laying his hands on each one, he healed them.

Moreover, demons came out of many people, shouting, "You are the Son of God!" But he rebuked them and would not allow them to speak, because they knew he was the Messiah.

GOING DEEPER

Capernaum, a small Jewish fishing village on the north edge of the Sea of Galilee, was the scene of constant activity. It was where Jesus at times lived, slept, and ate during his years of ministry. From that vantage point, Jesus visited other towns situated around the lake and inland to other parts of Galilee. He had compassion for the townspeople He met in His travels and healed many of their maladies with His touch.

On this particular occasion, as the evening approached, the end of Sabbath day was almost over. Jesus entered Capernaum. Tired from His travel, He was looking forward to a meal and rest.

A few days earlier Jesus had healed a man with leprosy. Although the man was warned not to tell anyone of his healing, it became evident by the crowd waiting for Jesus that the news had spread quickly. They trusted what they heard about Jesus and His healing powers. Among the inhabitants of the small town were fishermen, farmers, artisans, and merchants. The able-bodied had brought sick friends and relatives for healing. They had heard that Jesus had power over disease, demons, and infirmity.

When they found Jesus, they would call out to Him with the same need as the man with leprosy—the touch of the Master's hand. And then they would receive the same result: tender-hearted love that led to their healing.

PERSONAL REFLECTION

Just as the crowd in Capernaum trusted in Jesus, so can you. Jesus desires to be an active participant in every aspect of your life. If you trust in His goodness and put your faith in Him, He will be right beside you as you reach a goal on a mountaintop or as you persevere through a valley. Jesus calls you to continue in your faith walk no matter your current circumstance. Jesus is your example. He may have gotten weary, tired, and hungry, but He never failed to do the will of His Father. You do have access to the resource that is above all resources—Jesus Christ. He has given you work to accomplish on earth that only you can accomplish. Offer up your hands as a resource that He can use to do His work. In doing so, you will experience the joy of the touch of the Master's hand.

In what ways has Jesus' guiding touch influenced your life?

PRAYER

God of the Bible, thank you for revealing yourself through Jesus Christ. The truth has been made known to me through His words and miraculous works. May I always feel your guiding touch in my life and hear your words come forth from my soul.

Through your grace, you choose to bless and guide your children. Thank you for allowing us to bring petitions to your throne through intercessory prayer for all in need of your healing touch, your caring touch, your correcting touch, your wisdom, and your divine truth. There are so many needs and you are the great supplier of what people need. What a faithful blessing you are. We are grateful that we can always count on your loving touch no matter our circumstances. Amen.

TODAY'S TRUTH

JESUS HEALS BY HIS TOUCH AND HIS WORDS.

When Evening Comes

By C. K. Sharpe

They watched day vanish westward with the sun
Afternoon fading with Sabbath nearly done
Soon they'd seek in Capernaum Mary's Son
There He'd bear their burdens when evening comes.

The crowds did not know in a year or so they'd see
Jesus' stretched out arms and His bended knees
Nailed to a cross to bear their sins on Calvary's tree
There He'd bear their burdens when evening comes.

They watched day vanish westward with the sun
There He'd bear their burdens when evening comes.

Jesus Restores
a Demon-Possessed Man

The Miracle of Redemption

LUKE 8:26–39 NIV

They sailed to the region of the Gerasenes, which is across the lake from Galilee. When Jesus stepped ashore, he was met by a demon-possessed man from the town. For a long time this man had not worn clothes or lived in a house, but had lived in the tombs. When he saw Jesus, he cried out and fell at his feet, shouting at the top of his voice, "What do you want with me, Jesus, Son of the Most High God? I beg you, don't torture me!" For Jesus had commanded the impure spirit to come out of the man. Many times it had seized him, and though he was chained hand and foot and kept under guard, he had broken his chains and had been driven by the demon into solitary places.

Jesus asked him, "What is your name?"

"Legion," he replied, because many demons had gone into him. And they begged Jesus repeatedly not to order them to go into the Abyss.

A large herd of pigs was feeding there on the hillside. The demons begged Jesus to let them go into the pigs, and he gave them permission. When the demons came out of the man, they went into the pigs, and the herd rushed down the steep bank into the lake and was drowned.

When those tending the pigs saw what had happened, they ran off and reported this in the town and countryside, and the people went out to see what had happened. When they came to Jesus, they found the man from whom the demons had gone out, sitting at Jesus' feet, dressed and in his right mind; and they were afraid. Those who had seen it told the people how the demon-possessed man had been cured. Then all the people of the region of the Gerasenes asked Jesus to leave them, because they were overcome with fear. So he got into the boat and left.

The man from whom the demons had gone out begged to go with him, but Jesus sent him away, saying, "Return home and tell how much God has done for you." So the man went away and told all over town how much Jesus had done for him.

GOING DEEPER

A legion is no small number—an army six thousand strong. A man had been driven mad by a legion of demons, and he came to Jesus for help. Jesus took pity on the poor naked man who was overtaken by these evil spirits.

Jesus proved His redemptive power to the people watching when He sent the legion into the herd of pigs and then down a steep bank. Only God has the authority to do what He demonstrated that day to the Gerasenes. They realized then that He was not a miracle worker or a prophet, but that He was God.

No chains or shackles, invisible or otherwise (such as sex, drugs, alcohol, gambling, smoking, or any other destructive force such as jealousy, self-pity, guilt, and pride) can keep us from the peace and safety that God offers. We can be overcomers of satan's cruelties through the power of Jesus Christ. He can redeem us from our state of bondage. When we allow our soul to fill with His redemptive power, we receive the freedom that comes with it.

PERSONAL REFLECTION

If you become pressured by forces beyond your strength, look to the One in whom you can find refuge. That One is Jesus Christ. Your flesh may be weak, but He is strong. He is ready to redeem you no matter your circumstance.

If you need set free from a stronghold in your life, now is the time to break its chains. Depending on your situation, it may not be a journey without a struggle, but you know He will be right at your side. Have faith. God has the ultimate control over sin. Ask God for His redemption and release from the stronghold's grip.

Is there an area in your life you would like Jesus to take a hold of and break its chains?

PRAYER

Mighty Father, I know that when I call out to you in my weakness, you will hear me. I recognize I am helpless apart from what you do in my life. You tell me that as far as the east is from the west, you can remove my transgressions. I ask you to remove any bindings that may be separating me from the contentment I can have by living in your presence. May I keep my eyes on Jesus as I grow in faith and live the life you desire for me.

I'm ready. I thank you for favoring me with your loving act of redeeming grace. I want to walk in the freedom of your Kingdom life. Thank you, Lord, for the freedom I find in you. Amen.

TODAY'S TRUTH

JESUS' REDEMPTIVE POWER BREAKS THE CHAINS THAT BIND ONE'S LIFE.

Jesus Heals a Gentile Woman's Demon-Possessed Daughter

Miracle of Blessing Faith

MARK 7:24–30 NIV

Jesus left that place and went to the vicinity of Tyre. He entered a house and did not want anyone to know it; yet he could not keep his presence secret. In fact, as soon as she heard about him, a woman whose little daughter was possessed by an impure spirit came and fell at his feet. The woman was a Greek, born in Syrian Phoenicia. She begged Jesus to drive the demon out of her daughter.

"First let the children eat all they want," he told her, "for it is not right to take the children's bread and toss it to the dogs."

"Lord," she replied, "even the dogs under the table eat the children's crumbs."

Then he told her, "For such a reply, you may go; the demon has left your daughter."

She went home and found her child lying on the bed, and the demon gone.

GOING DEEPER

The tenacity of a mother! She wanted the health of her child back, and she was filled with so much hope, faith—and yes, tenacity—that she pressed Jesus to meet her need. An awful demon had overtaken her daughter's mind. She wanted Jesus to get rid of it.

No doubt she had probably heard of His merciful love of people. Jesus had been ministering to the Jewish community, so why wouldn't His love extend to her too?

What an illustration of faith. She went to the Lord with a faith so powerful that she was spiritually emboldened to claim a rightful place of petition at His feet. She was confident that Jesus would meet her need if she stayed the course and kept asking.

Because of her faithfulness and persistence, Jesus answered her prayer. There are times that God's answer is no to us because He has a greater purpose. In those times, He grants us grace to move on with our life.

The daughter received healing because of her mother's revealed faith—what a loving God we have.

PERSONAL REFLECTION

Perhaps you have a tenacious prayer life; that is, you are a person that keeps repeatedly praying for someone or for a particular result that is especially dear to your heart. Through God's sufficiency, even table scraps blessed by the Lord are enough to satisfy your deepest need. So, as a child of God, you can take your need confidently to the throne of mercy in prayer; emboldened by your faith, spiritually empowered to petition at Jesus' feet.

Jesus tested the tenacity and faithfulness of the Syrophoenician woman. According to God's will, He may take us through a humbling process as He did the desperate woman. You can be certain that He had a divine design for her life, and He has a divine plan for yours.

Tell of a time when you refused to give up praying for a particular need with certainty that God would hear and answer your faithful tenaciousness.

PRAYER

Dear Lord, thank you for your love for me. Thank you for letting me come boldly to your throne with worship, thanksgiving, and at times with tenacious petitions. Your power and love of people is known throughout your Word so I feel encouraged to boldly step out in faith and pray for the welfare or restoration of others.

I am grateful for your mercy in times when I become overly stubborn, relentless, and unshakable—in my personal life as well as my prayer life. May I always hold onto my faith with such a tenacity that you find my resolve unshakable.

May I always experience joy and peace as I trust you to answer my prayers according to your will and purpose. Amen.

TODAY'S TRUTH

GOD BLESSES FAITH IN ACTION.

Jesus Heals a Boy with a Demon

The Miracle of Developing Mountain Movers

MATTHEW 17:14–20 NIV

"When they came to the crowd, a man approached Jesus and knelt before him. "Lord, have mercy on my son," he said. "He has seizures and is suffering greatly. He often falls into the fire or into the water. I brought him to your disciples, but they could not heal him."

"You unbelieving and perverse generation," Jesus replied, "how long shall I stay with you? How long shall I put up with you? Bring the boy here to me." Jesus rebuked the demon, and it came out of the boy, and he was healed at that moment.

Then the disciples came to Jesus in private and asked, "Why couldn't we drive it out?"

He replied, "Because you have so little faith. Truly I tell you, if you have faith as small as a mustard seed, you can say to this mountain, 'Move from here to there,' and it will move. Nothing will be impossible for you."

GOING DEEPER

The disciples were dumbfounded! They weren't anywhere near ready to be called mountain movers as their Lord was insinuating they would be if they had enough faith in God. To remove mountains was a common expression in the Jewish culture that was usually reserved for a seasoned teacher that was superb at problem-solving and removing difficulties.

Although the disciples had been sent out to perform healing tasks on all kinds of sicknesses and diseases through God's power and they had been successful, they had not reached the level of faith required to remove this particular demon. It required a God-sized faith that the disciples did not have. They needed a faith that could remove mountains.

Jesus rebuked the spirit; it came out, and the boy was healed. This miracle became a teachable moment for the disciples. They received firsthand experience as to the magnitude that faithful prayer can play in the life of the redeemed.

If we pray with expectant faith, God will give us the means to overcome difficulties and rise above obstacles. We must keep vigilant in the study of God's Word and a disciplined prayer life to grow our faith. These exercises of faith will help us to stand against the evil darts of temptation and sin. The Bible and prayer are tremendous resources. Let's utilize them to His glory.

PERSONAL REFLECTION

Trials or events may come into your life from time to time that cause your faith to either stumble as it did for the disciples or to increase. Trials do not come to you for God's benefit, for God already knows the quantity and quality of your faith. Look at your next trial as an occasion to examine what motivates you and the strength of your faith. A trial gives us an opportunity to open God's Word and learn His truths and power; to become a mountain remover. His truths impart wisdom to us that enables us to endure our immediate hardship and become an overcomer. Trials can only come to you in whatever form God allows. Whatever your mountain is today, build your faith through God's truths and power so the mountain will move.

What mountain do you face today?

Prayer

God, you are the epitome of faithfulness. I count on the promises of your Word. I come to you with an expectant faith knowing you will provide the means to overcome difficulties and obstacles in my life. It is hard though, God, when I am going through the actual trial. In times of doubt, I find it uncomfortable to lean on you. I ask your forgiveness for my weaknesses.

Let me, through your strength, be found living in true and faithful perseverance. By living this way, may I be able to be an overcomer. I ask that you examine my heart regularly with hopes that you find it strong of faith. I want to grow and exercise my faith so that one day I might be called one of your mountain removers. In Jesus' holy name, amen.

TODAY'S TRUTH

JESUS DEVELOPS MOUNTAIN MOVERS.

Jesus Heals a Blind, Mute Demoniac

The Miracle of Unity

LUKE 11:14–28 NIV

Jesus was driving out a demon that was mute. When the demon left, the man who had been mute spoke, and the crowd was amazed. But some of them said, "By Beelzebul, the prince of demons, he is driving out demons." Others tested him by asking for a sign from heaven.

Jesus knew their thoughts and said to them: "Any kingdom divided against itself will be ruined, and a house divided against itself will fall. If Satan is divided against himself, how can his kingdom stand? I say this because you claim that I drive out demons by Beelzebul. Now if I drive out demons by Beelzebul, by whom do your followers drive them out? So then, they will be your judges. But if I drive out demons by the finger of God, then the kingdom of God has come upon you.

"When a strong man, fully armed, guards his own house, his possessions are safe. But when someone stronger attacks and overpowers him, he takes away the armor in which the man trusted and divides up his plunder.

"Whoever is not with me is against me, and whoever does not gather with me scatters.

"When an impure spirit comes out of a person, it goes

through arid places seeking rest and does not find it. Then it says, 'I will return to the house I left.' When it arrives, it finds the house swept clean and put in order. Then it goes and takes seven other spirits more wicked than itself, and they go in and live there. And the final condition of that person is worse than the first."

As Jesus was saying these things, a woman in the crowd called out, "Blessed is the mother who gave you birth and nursed you."

He replied, "Blessed rather are those who hear the word of God and obey it."

GOING DEEPER

Everyone has a beating heart. For most, it functions great without any thought about it. Valves allow blood to flow in one direction with each heartbeat and we count on these valves to direct our physical life blood through the chambers of our heart.

What happens if the heart is not spiritually working properly? Who controls our spiritual lifeblood? The answer—the Holy Spirit. He functions as our valves. He guides our heart in the right direction by warning us if it is being divided by evil. He guides our spiritual life in God's direction. He consciously tells us to open and close doors in our life that are not beneficial to our spiritual growth. In other words, He keeps sin's deteriorating properties from moving in and damaging our spiritual heart. He keeps us from having a divided heart.

Our *personal* goodness will not prevail when we stand before the Lord. It is impossible for the spiritual heart to flow in the wrong direction. The goal of evil is to divide us from the Kingdom of God; therefore, a house divided.

Just as Jesus drove out the demon in the mute, He can drive out sin from a contrite heart. God wants your whole heart, not a divided one. God is the mender of repentant hearts. He restores with His forgiveness. Only the one true living God can accomplish the repair work that is required.

PERSONAL REFLECTION

You also have a *power source* to keep your spiritual heart beating in God's direction. That power and authority comes from Jesus.

You know where your hope lies. Evil serves nothing more than to drive you into the arms of God, accomplishing the very opposite of its objective of separating you from Him.

Jesus' dramatic healing of the mute revealed who He was. The healing was an indication that Jesus had the power over the mute's life and the ability to forgive his sins. Salvation was there, and it was his choice to accept or reject it.

Jesus prevails in your journey through His love, mercy, and forgiveness of sin. You belong to Him and are destined to live in His Kingdom that is *united* in peace and love. Do you feel the beating of your heart as it quickens with thoughts of gratefulness?

What part of your heart needs cleaning out
so God can fill it up with His love?

PRAYER

As a child of God, when the deceiver tries to come into my heart and divide it, may he see that it is already full of you, and there is no room for his wickedness nor will there ever be room for anything else but you. Through the Holy Spirit may I stand firmly against sin and its deteriorating properties.

The Scripture tells me: "A good man brings good things out of the good stored up in his heart, and an evil man brings evil things out of the evil stored up in his heart. For the mouth speaks what the heart is full of." Thank you, Father, for this quick and easy way to tell if my heart is united in your love. May only your truth flow from my heart to my lips. In Jesus' name, amen.

TODAY'S TRUTH

A HOUSE UNITED IN JESUS STANDS FIRM AGAINST THE DECEIVER.

PART IV

RAISING
THE
DEAD

DAY 17

Jesus Raises a Widow's Son in Nain

The Miracle of His Life-Giving Words

LUKE 7:11–17 NIV

Soon afterward, Jesus went to a town called Nain, and his disciples and a large crowd went along with him. As he approached the town gate, a dead person was being carried out—the only son of his mother, and she was a widow. And a large crowd from the town was with her. When the Lord saw her, his heart went out to her and he said, "Don't cry."

Then he went up and touched the bier they were carrying him on, and the bearers stood still. He said, "Young man, I say to you, get up!" The dead man sat up and began to talk, and Jesus gave him back to his mother.

They were all filled with awe and praised God. "A great prophet has appeared among us," they said. "God has come to help his people." This news about Jesus spread throughout Judea and the surrounding country.

GOING DEEPER

The woman and her son experienced victory in Jesus. Death had seemed to have been a cruel victor to the mother in today's passage. Her circumstance was dire. She had not only lost her only son, but she had lost her lawful rights and support that her only child accorded her. Jesus saw; Jesus knew; Jesus had compassion.

The healing power of Jesus' life-giving words changed her day from one of mourning to one of joy. She would be able to take pleasure in her son once again.

There is victory through Jesus' life-giving words for us today. We find security in knowing there is an everlasting life waiting for us through Jesus. We know and trust that His words are words of life.

We have turned from sin and are becoming more and more like Jesus as we grow in His likeness. Through Jesus, we have been set apart for the use of our Creator, and through Him our sanctification process continues for a lifetime. Romans 6:22 is an encouraging verse in that it tells us, "But now that you have been set free from sin and have become slaves of God, the fruit you get leads to sanctification and its end, eternal life" (ESV).

The woman and son in our Scripture today experienced victory in Jesus through His life-giving words. Those we love and care for may leave us temporarily through death, but those souls who have victory through Jesus will be with Him forever. There is great comfort in knowing that.

PERSONAL REFLECTION

Has there been a time in your life when the tissue wadded in your hand could not hold one more tear? Grief is hard to overcome and it takes time. You can take comfort in knowing Jesus is there with you as you go through the grieving process. He is the great Comforter. God understands our grief because He too experienced sadness; the death of His Son on the cross.

We have a High Priest, One who hears our prayers, sees our tears, and sympathizes with them. His name is Jesus. By His death, we were reconciled to God. From His throne in heaven, He watches over you and prays for you. He intercedes for you. He stands before God on your behalf. Having seen your eyes pour out tears to God and knowing your heart, He pleads your case before the Father. He is your understanding friend; therefore, have hope. Be comforted knowing Jesus sees you, Jesus knows you, and Jesus intercedes for you.

In what ways does Jesus intercede for you?

PRAYER

Dear Lord, thank you for being my High Priest. I am grateful for your might and strength over death and the grave. I know my eternal life is secure through your death and resurrection.

When I am going through a period of grief, I thank you for your shoulder to lean on and the comfort I find in your Word.

Thank you, Jesus, for your righteousness and the Father who sees me through your eyes. Your grace knows no limits.

The widow had a crowd of people to support her in her grief. I want to thank you for my friends who come around me in times that I need comforting. Please bless my friends for their support and listening ears during my time of need, no matter the cause. In His name I pray, amen.

TODAY'S TRUTH

WE HAVE ETERNAL SECURITY THROUGH JESUS' LIFE-GIVING WORDS.

Jesus Raises Jairus' Daughter to Life
The Miracle of Hope

LUKE 8:49–56 NASB

While He was still speaking, someone came from the house of the synagogue official, saying, "Your daughter has died; do not trouble the Teacher anymore." But when Jesus heard this, He answered him, "Do not be afraid any longer; only believe, and she will be made well." When He came to the house, He did not allow anyone to enter with Him, except Peter and John and James, and the girl's father and mother. Now they were all weeping and lamenting for her; but He said, "Stop weeping, for she has not died, but is asleep." And they began laughing at Him, knowing that she had died. He, however, took her by the hand and called, saying, "Child, arise!" And her spirit returned, and she got up immediately; and He gave orders for something to be given her to eat. Her parents were amazed; but He instructed them to tell no one what had happened.

GOING DEEPER

As they entered Jairus' home where his daughter lay, the father's prayer shawl lay discarded on a chair in the corner of the room. The cloth was still damp where her father's tears had fallen on it a short time before. Many prayers by the family had called upon God to heal the little girl as she lay dying. They prayed for a miracle. Jesus was their only hope.

The synagogue leader went to Jesus, kneeling before Him and expressing his faith by requesting Jesus' healing touch for his daughter. Hadn't a woman just a few minutes ago received healing by touching Him? The father received word his daughter had died. Jesus overheard and told Jairus not to fear, but believe. The father held onto that hope that Jesus could help his daughter. And Jesus did. He brought her back to her mother and father.

It is a painful experience for anyone who has been by the bedside of a loved one whose time on earth is almost over. Death comes at its appointed time. We put our trust in Jesus. We claim His promise that one day He will raise up those who believe in Him. The Scripture is clear to explain that those indwelled by the Holy Spirit will have life given to the mortal body through His Spirit. What a glorious day that will be!

PERSONAL REFLECTION

The feeling of hopelessness and grief can be overwhelming as you deal with the loss of a loved one. Have hope, dear one. Cling to the One who heals the sick and raises the dead. Lean on your heavenly Father's shoulder as you journey through your grief. He is aware of your pain and will help you throught it.

Jesus gives hope to the living in that someday, all who see Jesus face-to-face shall in that instant become like Him. The apostle John encourages us in that belief, for he tells us that as beloved children, what we will be has not yet appeared, but when Jesus appears we shall be like Him. See 1 John 3:2 for this affirmation.

Someday, dear child of God, there will be a reuniting with your loved ones in heaven. We have a great hope and a great God.

How do you express hope in the resurrection?

PRAYER

Comforter of my heart, I lay my pain and sorrow at your feet. Thank you for being with me in my times of mourning—the death of a loved one, a miscarriage, divorce or loss of health, a job, retirement, financial instability, selling a home, or loss of a dear pet.

Let me feel your healing touch flooding my soul as Jairus' daughter did. Let me find joy in your word, as you ease my pain and replace it with your comforting words. Thank you for being with me as I go through difficult times. Thank you for drying my tears and consoling my grief. Amen.

TODAY'S TRUTH

WE HAVE HOPE THROUGH JESUS.

"Talitha cumi"*

By C. K. Sharpe

Her father's not ready to say good-bye.
He's gone for the Healer; He can't let her die
He runs and stumbles as tears cloud his eyes
Time's almost gone and his heart pleads this cry.

I'm not finished; I'm not letting her go
It's not your time, daughter, for this I know
There's singing and dancing and more to do
Heaven can wait awhile longer for you.

No pain lingers now upon her young brow
Mother holds her small hand as tears flow down
Jesus asked ones gathered why do you weep:
"The child is not dead, but only asleep."

I'm not finished; I'm not letting her go
It's not your time, daughter, for this I know
There's singing and dancing and more to do
Heaven can wait awhile longer for you.

* *"Little girl, I say to you, arise!"*

Jesus Raises Lazarus from the Dead
The Miracle of Revealing God's Glory

JOHN 11:30–46 NASB

Now Jesus had not yet come into the village, but was still in the place where Martha met Him. Then the Jews who were with her in the house, and consoling her, when they saw that Mary got up quickly and went out, they followed her, supposing that she was going to the tomb to weep there. Therefore, when Mary came where Jesus was, she saw Him, and fell at His feet, saying to Him, "Lord, if You had been here, my brother would not have died." When Jesus therefore saw her weeping, and the Jews who came with her also weeping, He was deeply moved in spirit and was troubled, and said, "Where have you laid him?" They said to Him, "Lord, come and see." Jesus wept. So the Jews were saying, "See how He loved him!" But some of them said, "Could not this man, who opened the eyes of the blind man, have kept this man also from dying?"

So Jesus, again being deeply moved within, came to the tomb. Now it was a cave, and a stone was lying against it. Jesus said, "Remove the stone." Martha, the sister of the deceased, said to Him, "Lord, by this time there will be a stench, for he has been dead four days." Jesus said to her, "Did I not say to you that if you believe, you will see the glory of God?" So they removed the stone. Then Jesus raised His eyes, and said, "Father, I thank You that You have heard Me. I knew that You always hear Me;

but because of the people standing around I said it, so that they may believe that You sent Me." When He had said these things, He cried out with a loud voice, "Lazarus, come forth." The man who had died came forth, bound hand and foot with wrappings, and his face was wrapped around with a cloth. Jesus said to them, "Unbind him, and let him go."

Therefore many of the Jews who came to Mary, and saw what He had done, believed in Him. But some of them went to the Pharisees and told them the things which Jesus had done.

Going Deeper

It had been several days since Lazarus' death, and his sisters' hope of him being healed vanquished with his passing. And so, they wept.

Mary and Martha probably didn't have a full understanding of God's glory. Jesus was about to make that connection for them, along with the many others standing around Lazarus' burial site.

Jesus wanted to display God's glory at the gravesite so all in attendance might be changed by it. Jesus wanted them to experience it through His timing and transforming power. People would be able to see, feel, and experience the might of God's glory. If you could package all His incommunicable attributes plus the ones He shares with us—mercy, love, knowledge, and others—we would have but a small glimpse of His character, His glory. What an awesome God we have!

Jesus did travel on to Bethany with a purpose. He did restore Lazarus back to perfect health, just not in the way the sisters expected. Jesus revealed His divine power through raising Lazarus. He showed the sovereignty and glory of God; He revealed Himself.

PERSONAL REFLECTION

God's glory is all around you.

To Mary and Martha and those at the gravesite, Jesus chose to display His glory through the resurrection of Lazarus. Jesus did it so it would be beneficial to them and later to us. Through this display of glory, Jesus revealed who He is (as recorded in John 11:27): "Jesus said to her, 'I am the resurrection and the life; he who believes in Me will live even if he dies, and everyone who lives and believes in Me will never die.'"

How does God reveal His glory to you?

PRAYER

Father, your glory is all around and is revealed in so many ways to your children. I ask you now to show the glory of your tender mercies by wrapping your arms around those that need to be comforted. As you bring caring people to those who may be weeping, please give them the right words to say, so they become a blessing to these hurting ones. And, when the time is right, have them share a sweet time of testimony for your glory. Thank you for being the Great Comforter of souls and wiping away the tears of the bereaved. Amen.

TODAY'S TRUTH

WHEN WE WEEP, JESUS WEEPS WITH US.

PART V

CURES

A Nobleman's Son Healed

The Miracle of Progressive Faith

JOHN 4:46–54

So Jesus came again to Cana of Galilee where He had made the water wine. And there was a certain nobleman whose son was sick at Capernaum. When he heard that Jesus had come out of Judea into Galilee, he went to Him and implored Him to come down and heal his son, for he was at the point of death. Then Jesus said to him, "Unless you people see signs and wonders, you will by no means believe."

The nobleman said to Him, "Sir, come down before my child dies!"

Jesus said to him, "Go your way; your son lives." So the man believed the word that Jesus spoke to him, and he went his way. And as he was now going down, his servants met him and told him, saying, "Your son lives!"

Then he inquired of them the hour when he got better. And they said to him, "Yesterday at the seventh hour the fever left him." So the father knew that it was at the same hour in which Jesus said to him, "Your son lives." And he himself believed, and his whole household.

This again is the second sign Jesus did when He had come out of Judea into Galilee.

GOING DEEPER

The father was frantic knowing that his power, wealth, high-ranking position, and well-connected friends in Capernaum could do nothing to save his son. Being one of King Herod's royal officials, he at times held power over someone's life or death, but he held no power that could alter the outcome for his son. The father felt hopeless. His son would soon die if nothing was done to save him.

His heart could not stand the pain of his child's suffering. Was there nothing he could do? He had heard of a miracle worker with divine powers staying about twenty miles away. Jesus was performing healings there, and he had heard talk of Jesus' love and compassion for others. But how could he humble himself to go seek out this man who didn't share the same customs or religion as he? He also heard this man claimed to be the Son of God.

Out of desperation, and a heart with only a little faith, he quickly made the long journey to Cana of Galilee to find this miracle worker. Once found, the nobleman faced Jesus with his problem. Jesus listened and grew the man's faith by responding, "Go ... your son lives." The official's faith turned from believing what Jesus could do to believing in who Jesus was.

PERSONAL REFLECTION

As a parent, you worry when your child catches a childhood illness. You make your youngster as comfortable as possible, administer the proper medicine, and pray to God, the Author and Ruler of the universe, for your child's return to health. Then you wait in faith as the temperature returns to normal. This act is an example of your faith in action, believing in the power and healing of your Lord.

You may not realize it, but others monitor your faith by how you act and react in your home and within your community. You are a Christlike witness, just as the king's royal official was after his son was healed. The official heard that Jesus was a man of healing and returned home knowing he had just been in the presence of God.

You also have that same influence within your household. What a blessing to have such an indwelling of the Holy Spirit. Your complete trust in Jesus is an inspiration to others that causes them to "want what you have."

How do you walk by faith?

PRAYER

Dear Lord, thank you for being the Great Physician, the Healer of body, mind, and soul. I thank you for your healing touch in times of sickness, your spirit of peace in times of mental anguish, and restoration of my soul in times of unrest. I count on your power and presence in my life. I am so pleased that you and the Father are one, for it is in you I trust for my salvation.

In faith, I have learned to believe without seeing as the nobleman did in returning home to find his son healed. This action is indeed the way faith looks. Thank you for your gift of healing that you administer in times of need. Amen.

TODAY'S TRUTH

FAITH BELIEVES BEFORE ANSWERED PRAYER.

Peter's Mother-in-Law Healed
The Miracle of Fullness of Life

MARK 1:29-31 NLT

After Jesus left the synagogue with James and John, they went to Simon and Andrew's home. Now Simon's mother-in-law was sick in bed with a high fever. They told Jesus about her right away. So he went to her bedside, took her by the hand, and helped her sit up. Then the fever left her, and she prepared a meal for them.

GOING DEEPER

Peter's mother-in-law was a spiritual woman and being of service to others was a natural outpouring in her life. Now here she lay, in bed with a high fever.

Mighty are Jesus' acts of love. He showed His affection and sympathy for Peter's ill mother-in-law by completely healing her to fullness of life and activity. Jesus, preeminent over all, stood over her and with a word and touch rebuked her fever. Once again, this instant healing demonstrated to His disciples that He was the one sent by God as foretold in the Scriptures.

She was the first woman that Jesus healed and the first woman to serve Him. Although she remains nameless, she is a wonderful example of servitude as shown by her immediate response to receiving healing. She instantly got up and prepared a meal for Jesus and His friends.

This woman was blessed with a loving, caring servant's heart. This caring servant allowed the love in her heart to flow straight into the grateful arms of its recipients. It does not serve one's self-interests, but the interests of others.

We can only imagine hearing God telling Peter's mother-in-law at her appointed time, "Well done, good and faithful servant."

Personal Reflections

Your home too can have access to the Great Healer of all afflictions. The Lord hears your intercessory prayers for returned health for those you love. When restoration comes according to His will, don't be surprised if it's your heart's desire to honor Him with more time spent in His service. Sometimes you might find yourself in a position where it feels uncomfortable to serve others, but learning to serve in humility is a start to becoming the servant God desires to represent His Kingdom. God will prepare and enable you for the task He has set before you. Don't miss out on the fullness of life God offers in the areas of service.

How do you currently serve others?

Prayer

Lord of all, thank you for your healing power over sickness and disease. I am grateful for the many times you have healed in my household. May I be found faithful to testifying of your glory through answered prayers.

I want to be a faithful servant as Peter's mother-in-law was in her life. May your love shine in and out and through the windows of my home as I extend Christlike hospitality to family, friends, and neighbors in my community. I always want to glow in the fullness of life I have found in you. I give you all the praise as you continue to direct me according to your will. In your mighty name Jesus, I pray, amen.

TODAY'S TRUTH

GOD OFFERS
FULLNESS OF LIFE.

DAY 22

Jesus Cleanses a Leper
The Miracle of Cleansing Power

LUKE 5:12–14

And it happened when He was in a certain city, that behold, a man who was full of leprosy saw Jesus; and he fell on his face and implored Him, saying, "Lord, if You are willing, You can make me clean."

Then He put out *His* hand and touched him, saying, "I am willing; be cleansed." Immediately the leprosy left him. And He charged him to tell no one, "But go and show yourself to the priest, and make an offering for your cleansing, as a testimony to them, just as Moses commanded."

GOING DEEPER

Leprosy is a repulsive disease. To the townspeople he was a picture of sin and defilement. He was a social outcast who had to identify himself as a leper and caution people when he was in their vicinity. The man was full of advanced stage leprosy, and yes, he *was* a desperate, pitiful man in need of Jesus' cleansing power.

As this disfigured man saw Jesus, he fell upon his knees before Him and begged to be made clean. It became very real to the leper that all things are under God's rule as he submitted to Jesus' sovereignty. The leper's humble approach honored Jesus when he expressed his request to receive Jesus' cleansing power. This leper's faith was apparent to all that watched him.

We probably would have been shocked to watch Jesus stretch out His hand and willingly touch this leprous man. Since it's impossibile to be clean and dirty at the same time, Jesus' touch instantly transformed him from unclean to spotless. This action showed and proved the deity of God.

This example of expectancy on the part of the leper confirms that we may come to the Lord for healing and forgiveness of sin, but first we must recognize the need for cleansing and forgiveness as the leper did.

PERSONAL REFLECTION

What would you think if people called out to you to move to the other side of the street to avoid their affliction? You may never see a leper during your life, but there are ones in pain and anguish walking among us today. Loved one, do not cross the street. As you have ears to hear and eyes to see, stretch out your hand to help those in need of restoration as Jesus did with the leper. You may be the vehicle God has chosen to guide this person to His cleansing power. Remember that God is the one who prepares you for such days as these. Individuals in agony, no matter the suffering, need love, compassion, and encouragement. Misery is never an easy thing to see or help with, but you are called to minister to them, tend to them, calm them, and pray for them. Look to God for guidance to show you how you can help. Be willing to touch them with the love of Jesus.

---

*How are you prepared to reach
others with God's cleansing power?*

PRAYER

Dear Jesus, the only true compassion, strength, and love comes from you, Lord. Thank you for the patience you have with me. Before my salvation I came before you as a leper in the sense that I called out to you for help, for your salvation. I lift up my heart to you asking you to fill me up with God-sized love for people afflicted with all sorts of suffering.

If it is your will, have me gently tell others you offer forgiveness and fullness of life through your deliverance. Guide me in ways that I can be a help as you heal broken hearts, bind up wounds, and ease pains and sorrows as you did with the leper. May your people become encouragers in the lives of others that are experiencing difficulty. With your guidance, may we sweep your words across the world to all in need of your cleansing power. Amen.

TODAY'S TRUTH

WE ARE CALLED TO
LOVE AND HELP OUR
NEIGHBORS.

Jesus Heals a Centurion Servant
The Miracle of Believing Without Seeing

LUKE 7:1–10

Now when He concluded all His sayings in the hearing of the people, He entered Capernaum. And a certain centurion's servant, who was dear to him, was sick and ready to die. So when he heard about Jesus, he sent elders of the Jews to Him, pleading with Him to come and heal his servant. And when they came to Jesus, they begged Him earnestly, saying that the one for whom He should do this was deserving, "for he loves our nation, and has built us a synagogue."

Then Jesus went with them. And when He was already not far from the house, the centurion sent friends to Him, saying to Him, "Lord, do not trouble Yourself, for I am not worthy that You should enter under my roof. Therefore I did not even think myself worthy to come to You. But say the word, and my servant will be healed. For I also am a man placed under authority, having soldiers under me. And I say to one, 'Go,' and he goes; and to another, 'Come,' and he comes; and to my servant, 'Do this,' and he does *it*."

When Jesus heard these things, He marveled at him, and turned around and said to the crowd that followed Him, "I say to you, I have not found such great faith, not even in Israel!" And those who were sent, returning to the house, found the servant well who had been sick.

GOING DEEPER

If a Roman governor or king was not passing through, the centurion was probably the highest-ranking Roman in the small Jewish town of Capernaum. He was the mayor, sheriff, judge, and jury. He knew Jewish law and customs as well as Roman law and customs.

The centurion had heard of Jesus, and he knew that Jesus could heal his servant. He felt unworthy. He also knew that if he met and talked to Jesus, it could be socially harmful to Jesus and might cause an uproar. The centurion could have sent soldiers to get Jesus, but instead sent Jewish elders to make his appeal. It was relayed humbly and simply.

As Jesus listened to the request for healing, He was astonished by the qualities of discipleship that this captain of guards displayed through the voice of others. The centurion had glorified God through his humility of unworthiness by sending others he held in higher regard than himself to make the request. The centurion's great faith was revealed when he declared he only needed Jesus' word for the servant to be healed. He believed without seeing.

By seeking Jesus, the centurion was, in essence, seeking out the Kingdom of God. His heart condition revealed that he valued others through the love he showed for his servant. This centurion was a man indeed that revealed characteristics of a true believer.

The centurion understood authority and had an amazing faith in Jesus' absolute authority. And because of that faith, Jesus granted his request.

PERSONAL REFLECTION

When you think about Jesus' absolute authority and who you are in Christ, it becomes easier to comprehend what remarkable faith the centurion had in Jesus. He petitioned Jesus with his request the best way he knew how, through others. His faith did not waver. He understood Jesus was who He said He was.

Today, you have His written Word so that you can believe in His Son and know for certain that He is who He says He is. You don't ever have to feel undeserving to bother Jesus nor do you have to send a representative to talk to Jesus on your behalf. You have an open invitation to His throne room anytime you like.

The last time you were before Jesus,
in what ways did He see your amazing faith?

PRAYER

King of all kings, please grant me the ability to wrap my heart around the extent of your Lordship just as the centurion did. What a man of unwavering faith. I desire that same type of amazing faith. I humbly thank you for allowing my faith to mature as I read through your Word and experience its anointing upon my life.

What a privilege it is to come before you with my worship, praise, and petitions anytime I want. What comfort I receive in knowing that you are always available and eager for me to come to you, Lord Jesus. Thank you for your faithfulness in my life. Amen.

TODAY'S TRUTH

AS WE TRUST WHO GOD IS, OUR FAITH GROWS.

DAY 24

Jesus Forgives and Heals a Paralytic
The Miracle of Forgiveness

MARK 2:1–12

And again He entered Capernaum after some days, and it was heard that He was in the house. Immediately many gathered together, so that there was no longer room to receive them, not even near the door. And He preached the word to them. Then they came to Him, bringing a paralytic who was carried by four men. And when they could not come near Him because of the crowd, they uncovered the roof where He was. So when they had broken through, they let down the bed on which the paralytic was lying.

When Jesus saw their faith, He said to the paralytic, "Son, your sins are forgiven you."

And some of the scribes were sitting there and reasoning in their hearts, "Why does this Man speak blasphemies like this? Who can forgive sins but God alone?"

But immediately, when Jesus perceived in His spirit that they reasoned thus within themselves, He said to them, "Why do you reason about these things in your hearts? Which is easier, to say to the paralytic, 'Your sins are forgiven you,' or to say, 'Arise, take up your bed and walk'? But that you may know that the

Son of Man has power on earth to forgive sins"—He said to the paralytic, "I say to you, arise, take up your bed, and go to your house." Immediately he arose, took up the bed, and went out in the presence of them all, so that all were amazed and glorified God, saying, "We never saw anything like this!"

GOING DEEPER

It was a very contentious time in which Jesus ministered. The regions surrounding Jerusalem, including Samaria, Jordan, Perea, and Capernaum were becoming more and more agitated because of rumors circulating about Jesus. These rumors implied Jesus was infringing on the authority of the Jewish leadership. So it was on this day in Capernaum when Jesus was confronted with the paralytic lowered on a bed from a rooftop where He was speaking.

The paralytic's faith barometer was not readily obvious. In this paralytic's case, the cultural beliefs of the day were equal to what *society* found acceptable. For him, the belief was that his sin caused his paralysis. We know he was a man born into sin, but only God knew the true extent of the man's sin.

When Jesus forgave the man's sins instead of healing him as his four friends had hoped, the paralytic was satisfied. Certainly, this forgiveness of sin would upgrade his social standing within the community.

However, the religious leaders in attendance did not find Jesus' actions or speech acceptable. *No one but God could forgive sins.* Because of their self-righteous attitudes, the paralytic benefited. Jesus not only forgave the man his sins but healed him as well.

The paralytic's faith-filled friends were joyous. They had been a small part of helping him to a better life by bringing him to Jesus. Today, our true friends make us better people also. They too can guide us lovingly through God's Word, straight to Jesus.

PERSONAL REFLECTIONS

I forgive you. These are three powerful words that can either make or break your day. Hearing these words can bring restoration to you when you are upset. By saying these words to another, it brings reconciliation and resolution. These words are beneficial—their use results in spiritual advancement for all involved. For you choose, of your own free will, to forgive or to be forgiven.

"Son, your sins are forgiven" brought peace to the paralytic and later healing and salvation. Forgiveness is powerful. Just as God provided good spiritual friends to the paralytic, the Lord will surround you with the right relationships. Ask Jesus to bring friends into your life that would carry your *bed* if needed.

How has forgiveness brought peace and healing into your life?

PRAYER

Dear Lord, how great thou art. Thank you for forgiving my sins. I want to give you all the praise for the special relationship I have with you. I have picked up my spiritual bed, and my desire is to walk in your ways and live according to your Word.

I am grateful for friends that you have brought into my life. I especially want to thank you for those that helped with the "As iron sharpens iron, so one man sharpens another" process. May my friends and I be in constant fellowship with one another. Help me be a good, godly friend to someone today. Amen.

TODAY'S TRUTH

JESUS' FORGIVENESS HEALS.

Faith of Four

By C. K. Sharpe

There was no room to receive them,
Crowds surrounded the entrance door.
What could they do for him
These men who numbered four?

Their helpless friend was lying
Upon a paralytic's bed.
They couldn't reach Jesus for healing
So they took him to the rooftop instead.

They could hear the Master preaching
The good news from inside.
Many were listening to His teaching
As four climbed the stairs outside.

They dug clay slabs from the roof that day,
Enough to lower their friend to the floor.
They wouldn't have had to do it that way
If they could have gotten him through that door!

Jesus Heals a Man's Withered Hand

The Miracle of His Goodness

LUKE 6:6–11

Now it happened on another Sabbath, also, that He entered the synagogue and taught. And a man was there whose right hand was withered. So the scribes and Pharisees watched Him closely, whether He would heal on the Sabbath, that they might find an accusation against Him. But He knew their thoughts, and said to the man who had the withered hand, "Arise and stand here." And he arose and stood. Then Jesus said to them, "I will ask you one thing: Is it lawful on the Sabbath to do good or to do evil, to save life or to destroy?" And when He had looked around at them all, He said to the man, "Stretch out your hand." And he did so, and his hand was restored as whole as the other. But they were filled with rage, and discussed with one another what they might do to Jesus.

GOING DEEPER

Life is full of choices. Jesus decided that no matter what the scribes and Pharisees thought or did, He was going to restore the hand of the man of faith on this Sabbath day. This man came to learn from Jesus, not knowing he was going to be the instrument used in the Lord's teaching.

It was Jesus' decision to do good by healing this man's withered hand on this Sabbath day. His healing gave evidence that the Sadducees and Pharisees' restrictive rules on the Sabbath had grossly distorted the spirit and letter of the Law.

Jesus' goodness and His words heal *every day* of the week. He encourages us not to be overcome by evil but overcome evil with good. We decide to walk in His integrity every day. God wants us to show goodness because He is good, and He wants us to be like Him. Every sin and every *good* deed impact our life. Choosing good honors the one true God who is sovereign over all.

The Lord demonstrated that works of necessity are allowed on Sabbath, but we must never forget whose day it is—His day. We must spend it in His service and to His honor.

PERSONAL REFLECTION

Each day, you are faced with choices, good and bad. You weed out information that comes into your home, discern products you purchase, and choose between a myriad of other things that require filtering such as movies, radio stations, and reading materials. Choose to walk in His goodness. If you make a wrong decision, seek forgiveness through prayer, and continue to walk with Jesus.

Enjoy your Sabbath by worshiping and fellowshipping with your Lord. By all means, rest on this special day that He has provided you.

How do you honor the Lord on His day of rest?

PRAYER

Maker of all, what would I do without your examples of goodness in the Bible. Your love and compassion are beyond compare. Everything you do is for the benefit of teaching and admonishing for your glory and our good. Take whatever little goodness is inside of me and grow it to be used for your Kingdom.

On the Sabbath day, I choose to worship, sing, and praise you, Lord, for your truth and goodness. As the crippled man did, let me always stretch out my hands to you as I praise and pray to you. I know when I have decisions to make, you will place your wisdom right back into my outstretched hands. Amen.

TODAY'S TRUTH

GOD IS THE AUTHOR AND GIVER OF ALL GOOD THINGS.

Jesus Heals a Woman in a Crowd
The Miracle of Truth

LUKE 8:43–48

Now a woman, having a flow of blood for twelve years, who had spent all her livelihood on physicians and could not be healed by any, came from behind and touched the border of His garment. And immediately her flow of blood stopped.

And Jesus said, "Who touched Me?"

When all denied it, Peter and those with him said, "Master, the multitudes throng and press You, and You say, 'Who touched Me?'"

But Jesus said, "Somebody touched Me, for I perceived power going out from Me." Now when the woman saw that she was not hidden, she came trembling; and falling down before Him, she declared to Him in the presence of all the people the reason she had touched Him and how she was healed immediately.

And He said to her, "Daughter, be of good cheer; your faith has made you well. Go in peace."

GOING DEEPER

She was lonely. She had certainly been living with feelings of aloneness for some twelve years due to her affliction. She was an outcast in the community. She had gone to many physicians and tried numerous medicines to cure her issue of blood. Nothing helped, and she was tired.

Inching her way through the crowds, she followed Jesus. She knew people would be angry if she accidentally touched them, for they thought that her touch would make them unclean. Yet this woman knew that if she could just lay her hand on His clothing, she would be made well. Surely there was no harm in just a touch. So—she touched Him.

Jesus felt her touch. He knew she had faith, but she hadn't used it correctly. There was no need for her to take a blessing from Him. The Lord admonished her by calling her out in front of the crowd. Trembling, in truth, she confessed she had touched His garment. Her rightfully placed faith and truthfulness were rewarded with salvation.

If she had succeeded in disappearing after her healing, she would never have heard Jesus' last endearment to her. He called her "Daughter"—the only woman in the Bible that Jesus addressed this way. What a divine approval.

In those few moments, Jesus taught her that her confession of faith, not her touch, had been the healing power over her ailment. Salvation had indeed come to her that day.

PERSONAL REFLECTION

Blessed one, you have no need to tremble when you approach Jesus' throne. Remember how Jesus let His blood flow on Calvary so that you might be healed eternally through Him. He bled for you; He died for you. He was atonement for your sins. *Salvation comes to you.* Your desire should be to ask God, in truth, for healing. Have faith that He is at work and trust Him for the outcome.

If fear tries to creep in and interrupt you, remember, "Perfect love drives out fear"—and God loves us perfectly. Jesus forgave the woman with blood issues. Healing came to her through her truthful confession and *salvation came to her through her faith.*

---

*What have you confessed to the Lord
that may have caused you to tremble?*

PRAYER

Lord, the Healer of the afflicted and the remover of sin from the struggling heart, thank you for this woman with an issue of blood. Through your interaction with her, I learned I could pour out my heart to you in truthful confession and not be anxious. Thank you for letting me come to you with my problems.

Your great love never fails to overwhelm me. With tears of gratitude, I think about your shed blood at the cross. I am so glad there is no barrier between you and me; that it was removed at the cross. Thank you for your never-ending love and your touch in my life. Amen.

TODAY'S TRUTH

JESUS ALWAYS
LOVES US IN TRUTH;
WE NEED NOT FEAR.

Jesus Heals Two Blind Men

The Miracle of Sight

MATTHEW 9:27–31

When Jesus departed from there, two blind men followed Him, crying out and saying, "Son of David, have mercy on us!"

And when He had come into the house, the blind men came to Him. And Jesus said to them, "Do you believe that I am able to do this?"

They said to Him, "Yes, Lord."

Then He touched their eyes, saying, "According to your faith let it be to you." And their eyes were opened. And Jesus sternly warned them, saying, "See that no one knows it." But when they had departed, they spread the news about Him in all that country.

GOING DEEPER

Two men, both blind, did not have the slightest hope of ever seeing their shadows. Total darkness. But in their darkness, they believed Jesus to be the Son of David, the Messiah. They knew Jesus could cure their blindness if only they would ask. These two men possessed spiritual understanding and faith. They understood the word of the One who declared, "I am the light of the world. He who follows Me shall not walk in darkness, but

PART V - CURES

have the light of life" (John 8:12). They believed it, so they did exactly that; they followed Him.

He rewarded their faith with the gift of sight, and they were overjoyed. They could not help but share the good news of their miraculous healing. Their salvation had brought them illumination.

In today's society, unbelief is a form of blindness. A non-believer can't grasp or see spiritual reality. Only God's light can penetrate the darkness. As Christians, we are to let His light shine through us. We have been called, dear believers, not to hide our light under a bushel basket, but let it shine, shine, shine for the One that deserves our praise and adoration. Let others see it glow.

PERSONAL REFLECTION

As we allow our light to shine for Jesus, we will draw others to the light, just like a moth to a flame. Make sure you are not attracting others to you, but to the one real source of light, Jesus.

As others see your witness of lifestyle, love for others, and the fruit of the Spirit working out through your life, perhaps they will become ready for a light of their own. When they are ready, pray with them for Jesus to remove the darkness and unbelief from their life so Jesus' salvation glow may turn into a bright shining witness for His glory.

In what situations do you call upon Jesus to give you eyes to see spiritual truth?

PRAYER

Lord of heaven, thanks for bringing light into a dimming world through your people. Help me, Lord, to see you clearly, to let my light of faith shine on all who cross my path today; so I may be a testimony of your grace in my life.

The two blind men couldn't contain what you had done for them any more than I can hide the joy of my salvation. I am blessed to have a great God that entrusts me, through His grace, to light up the world with His Word. In my Savior's name I pray, amen.

TODAY'S TRUTH

JESUS GIVES PRACTICAL HELP TO THOSE WHO ASK.

Mercy for Two

By C. K. Sharpe

Hope of seeing shadows dark is hoped for no more;
Ne'er to see shadows pass while sitting at gates door.
Two men humbly begging their way through sightless life;
Hands outstretched for gifts, kind acts, pity for their strife.
Though rift of sight these two were blessed with faith-filled
  hearts;
Faith, steadfast friend, guiding through years of darkest dark.

Hope of seeing shadows dark is hoped for no more;
Ne'er to see shadows pass while sitting at gates door.
Humanity of Christ heard their insistent cries;
Though blind of eyes their voices could not be denied.
They begged Him to restore them with His healing grace;
He touched their eyes and then they saw God face-to-face.

Hope of seeing shadows dark is hoped for no more.

A Man Born Blind Receives Sight

The Miracle of Purpose

JOHN 9:1–12

Now as Jesus passed by, He saw a man who was blind from birth. And His disciples asked Him, saying, "Rabbi, who sinned, this man or his parents, that he was born blind?"

Jesus answered, "Neither this man nor his parents sinned, but that the works of God should be revealed in him. I must work the works of Him who sent Me while it is day; the night is coming when no one can work. As long as I am in the world, I am the light of the world."

When He had said these things, He spat on the ground and made clay with the saliva; and He anointed the eyes of the blind man with the clay. And He said to him, "Go, wash in the pool of Siloam" (which is translated, Sent). So he went and washed, and came back seeing.

Therefore the neighbors and those who previously had seen that he was blind said, "Is not this he who sat and begged?"

Some said, "This is he." Others said, "He is like him."

He said, "I am he."

Therefore they said to him, "How were your eyes opened?"

He answered and said, "A Man called Jesus made clay and anointed my eyes and said to me, 'Go to the pool of Siloam and wash.' So I went and washed, and I received sight."

Then they said to him, "Where is He?"
He said, "I do not know."

GOING DEEPER

Blindness is mentioned many times in the Old and New Testament. The Law said that the sins of the people could cause consequences for generations. For this man, Jesus said it was not so. This man born with blindness provided Jesus the opportunities to bless the unfortunate and teach the disciples as well.

Jesus had a purpose for this blind man. Through his healing, Jesus planned to reveal Himself to the disciples as the Son of God, who had come in the flesh. Jesus was working more closely with His disciples now in preparation for their task ahead; to preach and teach the *good news*. They needed to know without a doubt He was the Son of God.

Jesus also used this blind man as a lesson in faith and obedience. Jesus didn't use the spittle as the healing agent to restore sight but wanted to use something familiar to the man so as to encourage his belief in Jesus. (Saliva was a well-known medical home remedy.) On this particular Holy Day, Jesus was encouraging this man's faith and obedience.

It was God's power alone that brought light into this man's world. The healed man grew to recognize the Lordship of Jesus. As he interacted with people that day, the blind man's faith grew. He first addressed Jesus as a man, later as a prophet, then as Sir, and last and appropriately, Lord. He believed. Salvation had come. The restored man went away with eyes that had seen the true light.

PERSONAL REFLECTION

The amount of your faith does not limit the living God in carrying out His purpose for your life. However, it is your responsibility to walk in obedience according to His Word. The Lord's miraculous act that day was not for the glory of the man born blind but for God's glory and purpose. He was not blind because of anyone's sin but rather for the purpose of showing God's glory. The purpose was to show the works of God and reveal His Lordship.

God has you right where you are for a reason. His purpose may not be clear to you now, but as time passes you will realize that His intention for your life is uniquely planned for you and no one else. Only you can finish the work He has purposed especially for you.

---

*What do you think God's purpose
for your life is right now?*

PRAYER

Thank you for being the Light of the world which allows your children to see and follow you according to your purpose. Father, help me to know you better. My conscience lets me know when I am doing right or wrong, and since I have been saved, the Holy Spirit guides my life through your Word. Help me to heed the voice of the Holy Spirit and keep faithfully in your Word so that I am able to fulfill the purpose you have planned for me.

When I stumble in my spiritual blindness, I ask your for-giveness. May you see my desire for obedience being worked out in my life and my faith increasing accordingly. Amen.

TODAY'S TRUTH

FOLLOWING HIS
PURPOSE LEADS YOU
INTO HIS LIGHT.

A Mute Man Speaks

The Miracle of Speech

MATTHEW 9:32–34

As they went out, behold, they brought to Him a man, mute and demon-possessed. And when the demon was cast out, the mute spoke. And the multitudes marveled, saying, "It was never seen like this in Israel!"

But the Pharisees said, "He casts out demons by the ruler of the demons."

GOING DEEPER

Careless words hurt. Will the power of the tongue be deadly or loving today? This is a choice that we have to make as we speak our first words in the morning. First words from the mute after the demon was cast out, hopefully, were words of thanksgiving and praise for what the Lord had just done for him.

Words of destruction can spread, and spread rapidly, beyond the initial unkind words. The power of the tongue is the vessel by which temper, intolerance, and gossip can escape. We know gossip is a favorite tool used by the devil. Relationships can be broken due to gossip.

Let us rejoice in the words of our Lord as He tells us in 1 Peter 3:10–11, "He who would love life and see good days, let him refrain his tongue from evil, and his lips from speaking deceit. Let him turn away from evil and do good; let him seek peace and pursue it."

As the sun shines upon the day, we should greet each person we meet with God's "Son" shine. Loving words can make a dear one or a stranger's day happier. It's a blessing to use our tongue to give the Son our praise and glory. Now that's something worth spreading around.

PERSONAL REFLECTION

Will our words be deadly or loving today? Just know that our sensibilities can be challenged throughout our day. The words we speak are a matter of self-control. It can be defeated so easily by carelessness.

As we quickly ask God for His guidance and peace upon every situation before we answer, in due course, we will find His calm filling our hearts We are to be gracious as our Lord is gracious. Our tongue is to speak of life through Him, and truth of His word. Spoken words reveal a lot.

---

*In what areas do you want
to control your tongue better?*

PRAYER

Dear Father, bless you for giving me a tongue. Help me to use it wisely for your glory. I have been told that life and death are in the power of the tongue. May I use my tongue to speak of your life and truth. Please forgive me when I have used my speech in an unwise way. Give me courage to ask forgiveness of others for such offense.

Please help me to think and speak only what is profitable and beneficial to you. As the mute was freed from his silence, may you free your people from the burden of uncensored speech so that we may be found pleasing to you. In Jesus' name I pray, amen.

TODAY'S TRUTH

JESUS GAVE US A TONGUE SO WE CAN SPEAK OF HIS LIFE, HOPE, AND TRUTH.

Jesus Heals an Invalid at Bethesda
The Miracle of Listening and Responding

JOHN 5:1–15

After this there was a feast of the Jews, and Jesus went up to Jerusalem. Now there is in Jerusalem by the Sheep Gate a pool, which is called in Hebrew, Bethesda, having five porches. In these lay a great multitude of sick people, blind, lame, paralyzed, waiting for the moving of the water. For an angel went down at a certain time into the pool and stirred up the water; then whoever stepped in first, after the stirring of the water, was made well of whatever disease he had. Now a certain man was there who had an infirmity thirty-eight years. When Jesus saw him lying there, and knew that he already had been in that condition a long time, He said to him, "Do you want to be made well?"

The sick man answered Him, "Sir, I have no man to put me into the pool when the water is stirred up; but while I am coming, another steps down before me."

Jesus said to him, "Rise, take up your bed and walk." And immediately the man was made well, took up his bed, and walked.

And that day was the Sabbath. The Jews therefore said to him who was cured, "It is the Sabbath; it is not lawful for you to carry your bed."

He answered them, "He who made me well said to me, 'Take up your bed and walk.'"

Then they asked him, "Who is the Man who said to you, 'Take up your bed and walk'?" But the one who was healed did not know who it was, for Jesus had withdrawn, a multitude being in that place. Afterward Jesus found him in the temple, and said to him, "See, you have been made well. Sin no more, lest a worse thing come upon you."

The man departed and told the Jews that it was Jesus who had made him well.

GOING DEEPER

God knew the innermost thoughts of the infirmed man lying by Bethesda's pool—He was aware that this man was full of excuses, yet God also knew the crippled's heart. He desired to be healed.

Jesus' grace is simply amazing toward this man. First, He restores the natural man by saying, "Rise, take up your bed and walk." The man listened and responded to Jesus' request. When he was questioned later by the Jewish leaders about carrying his mat on the Sabbath, the previously crippled man blamed Jesus.

Jesus loves each of us and wants the best for us. It is His desire to restore us to full physical and spiritual health. He blesses us with undeserved acts of kindness and favor, just like He did for the invalid. *He desires that our body be brought into His wellness.*

Second, Jesus finds the man in the temple, restores Him spiritually, and makes it clear to him to sin no more. This action is a prime example of Jesus taking a troubled, excuse-filled life and making it whole. God blesses us today with His salvation message. *He desires that our soul is brought into His fullness.*

As the invalid was told to sin no more, we too are told to abide in Christ and not sin. Through our Lord, we will be victorious.

PERSONAL REFLECTION

The invalid had to recognize the Master's voice, listen, and then stand up and walk. It is the same with your relationship with God today. He talks, you listen. Jesus speaks to you in a way that is uniquely yours; but often times, His Word is the means through which He speaks.

Your interaction with Him is important to the Lord. Through prayer, you have a direct line of communication with Jesus. You talk, He listens. Then it's your time to rest in Him. For the answer will come according to His will and timing. Trust Him. He knows what is best for you.

Listen for His voice. He will tell you when it is time *to rise*. When you hear it, respond quickly and walk in His will. Listen, His dear one, listen.

---

*In what way do you listen
and respond when Jesus speaks?*

PRAYER

Lord, how gracious you are. You granted the invalid two miracles; one physically and one spiritually. Both healings were undeserved, both given to him in love. I am so glad I have a loving God who sees potential in humanity.

Take my life, Jesus, as it is today and make it wholly yours, spiritually and physically, as you did for the invalid at the Bethesda pool. I too do not deserve your favor.

When I hear your voice, I will listen, get up, and walk in your ways for I desire to be obedient to the word of the living God. Amen.

TODAY'S TRUTH

GOD HEARS US
AND WE HEAR HIM.

Jesus Heals Many Sick in Gennesaret

The Miracle of His Touch

MARK 6:53–56 KJV

And when they had passed over, they came into the land of Gennesaret, and drew to the shore.

And when they were come out of the ship, straightway they knew him,

And ran through that whole region round about, and began to carry about in beds those that were sick, where they heard he was.

And whithersoever he entered, into villages, or cities, or country, they laid the sick in the streets, and besought him that they might touch if it were but the border of his garment: and as many as touched him were made whole.

GOING DEEPER

Jesus' boat had anchored at the nothwest shore known as the Paradise of Galilee, and there was no time for the boy to waste. His father had sent him to bring his uncle to the shore. His uncle's leg had been injured in a work accident, and he probably would never walk again without the help of his crudely constructed crutch. The boy burst into his uncle's home and quickly explained where they needed to go for healing. Today his uncle would receive the healing touch of Jesus.

As Jesus walked along the shore, He was surrounded by Gennesaret inhabitants, as well as others who had heard or witnessed His miracles during the previous few days. The people of Gennesaret had faith, enough faith to know that Jesus was the well-known Healer of man. They had enough faith in the stories they heard to know that Jesus healed many disorders.

As the people laid their ailing in the area marketplaces for healing, Jesus saw hope in their eyes. Through His mercy, physical healing came to all who sought it. If only they would have realized that spiritual salvation was within their grasp, but on that day they asked only for physical healing.

Jesus, through His teaching and healing, laid the spiritual groundwork for those that sought Him. The love and hope that He saw in them brought them a step closer to opening their hearts to an ultimate healing experience; a spiritual one.

PERSONAL REFLECTION

When you are genuinely interested in people, they recognize and respond to you. When the people of Gennesaret brought their sick for healing, Jesus saw their love and hope for each other. They, in turn, had heard of His miraculous healings and knew that He would meet their physical needs. All they needed to do was ask and they would receive His healing touch.

Jesus sees your responses of kindness and your level of desire to do what you can for others. What wonderful things you can accomplish when you use your touch to further the Kingdom of God. Someone, somewhere, with hope in their heart, is in need of a caring touch today. Allow the Lord to use you to reach others with His Word, so they too can experience the touch of Jesus.

How do you want God to lay the groundwork of salvation through your touch?

PRAYER

Lord, I am glad you are about the business of changing hearts. Thank you for changing my heart's condition. You took my sin-filled heart and made it new in the spirit. Thank you for a heart that desires to be filled up with compassion; a heart that wants to help and tell others about you. Thank you for enriching my life with your words and touch.

I approach you with an expectant faith. Allow me to lay the groundwork of salvation for others according to your will; to plant your seed. Give me the right words to express that you are a God that changes hearts onto salvation. In your name, I pray, amen.

TODAY'S TRUTH

YOUR TOUCH DRAWS OTHERS TO JESUS.

Letter: Body Over Soul

By C. K. Sharpe

Beautiful Gennesaret,

To lost souls living in the tropical sun, dancing among palms, figs, olives, and grapes, don't you know time is but fleeting moments? One by one they go, taking the chance of redemption with them.

Beautiful Gennesaret,

You choose not to bow your head and examine within but cling to your outward beauty. Turn inward while there is still time. Search your hearts; true healing may yet come to you.

For now, you seek only physical restoration by the Master's touch or restoration His garment provides. Once healed, you have found no need for spiritual cleansing.

Beautiful Gennesaret,

Jesus' heart aches for the little faith He found in you.

Yours for the asking,
Salvation

Jesus Heals a Deaf-Mute
The Miracle of Communication

MARK 7:31–37

Again, departing from the region of Tyre and Sidon, He came through the midst of the region of Decapolis to the Sea of Galilee. Then they brought to Him one who was deaf and had an impediment in his speech, and they begged Him to put His hand on him. And He took him aside from the multitude, and put His fingers in his ears, and He spat and touched his tongue. Then, looking up to heaven, He sighed, and said to him, "Ephphatha," that is, "Be opened."

Immediately his ears were opened, and the impediment of his tongue was loosed, and he spoke plainly. Then He commanded them that they should tell no one; but the more He commanded them, the more widely they proclaimed *it*. And they were astonished beyond measure, saying, "He has done all things well. He makes both the deaf to hear and the mute to speak."

GOING DEEPER

He couldn't hear. His speech was unintelligible. It is hard to comprehend the loneliness, suffering, or sadness this man must have endured. He couldn't express himself adequately because of his physical weaknesses. However, communication drove his thoughts; for he did try to communicate through his garbled speech. He went with his friends to seek out the help of Jesus.

How wonderful is our Lord. Jesus understood this man's feelings of despair. He could have spoken a word, and the word would have healed the man. However, Jesus chose to take the man, and most likely those that had brought him, to a private place. The healing was very visual, very personal, very one-on-one. The man probably watched Jesus look up to heaven. Although he didn't hear Jesus' compassionate sigh of emotion or the tender words of healing, the deaf-mute could feel the gentle touch of his healer's fingers in his ears and the curative touch on his tongue. What a blessing this man experienced, realizing something wonderful was happening to him.

His encounter was so vivid, so real, and an encouragement to all that witnessed it. How could they keep this extraordinary restoration, this miracle, a secret? They couldn't; they didn't. They were so full of gratitude for what Jesus had done. The now hearing, now speaking man had received the grace of the Lord. They wanted everyone to know about it.

PERSONAL REFLECTION

Jesus has a unique, personal, and meaningful sign language for you. He used His fingers and touch to communicate His love and care for the deaf-mute. He shows His love and care to you by creating you in His likeness, by sustaining you with life, by providing the joy of salvation, and making you a member of His family.

We can also use our own special sign language to communicate with Him without using our words, but our actions. We can show our language by giving of ourselves in service to Him, by reading His Word, by praying regularly, and by loving our neighbors. That's a great sign to Him of our love and commitment to Him.

There is no doubt that His love surpasses our understanding, but one thing we know for sure, it's an everlasting love. He has given us many types of communication to prove it.

> *What type of unique sign language
> does Jesus use to talk to you?*

PRAYER

Father, thank you, for ears that hear and the ability to communicate through speech. Help me to use my spiritual ears (what my heart has heard) and my natural ears (what I have heard) to understand the truth of your Word.

Help me to use my speech to glorify you. As I open the Bible, let my eyes feast upon its bounty and hear the sound of your voice through your Scriptures. Your Word is alive and through your will, I can speak of your words to others. Thank you, Lord, that you communicate to your people through the Holy Spirit and your precious Word. Amen.

TODAY'S TRUTH

USE YOUR EARS
AND TONGUE FOR
GOD'S GLORY.

Jesus Heals a Crippled Woman

The Miracle of Sabbath Worship

LUKE 13:10–17

Now He was teaching in one of the synagogues on the Sabbath. And behold, there was a woman who had a spirit of infirmity eighteen years, and was bent over and could in no way raise herself up. But when Jesus saw her, He called her to Him and said to her, "Woman, you are loosed from your infirmity." And He laid His hands on her, and immediately she was made straight, and glorified God.

But the ruler of the synagogue answered with indignation, because Jesus had healed on the Sabbath; and he said to the crowd, "There are six days on which men ought to work; therefore come and be healed on them, and not on the Sabbath day."

The Lord then answered him and said, "Hypocrite! Does not each one of you on the Sabbath loose his ox or donkey from the stall, and lead it away to water it? So ought not this woman, being a daughter of Abraham, whom Satan has bound—think of it—for eighteen years, be loosed from this bond on the Sabbath?" And when He said these things, all His adversaries were put to shame; and all the multitude rejoiced for all the glorious things that were done by Him.

GOING DEEPER

Nothing could stop her from worshipping her Lord, not even her deformed, bent over body. This unnamed woman didn't let her physical challenge stop her from going to the synagogue on the Sabbath.

Surely her severely bent over form posed all sorts of problems. Everyday tasks would be challenging—imagine getting dressed. Health wise, it had to cause a lot of stress on her body. Worst of all, she was forced to spend her life looking down at the ground. She never could look at another person face-to-face or easily see God's beautiful world.

She went to worship that Sabbath with her physical infirmity and left glorifying God in her wellness, made perfect by the grace of Jesus. For it was God who chose to heal her that day. She had come to the synagogue to worship, not be physically healed. It was He who had called out to her. What a blessing! Her day of deliverance had come through the work of the One she worshiped each Sabbath.

Scripture tells us that those who remain steadfast under trial are blessed. Overcomers will receive the crown of life, which God has promised to those who love Him. Even though we may spend our lives going through painful periods or a lifetime of infirmity, may we always choose to carry our love for the Lord straight into eternity.

PERSONAL REFLECTION

As you go through trials, persecution, or infirmities, be encouraged and persevere through them with the help of Jesus. Seek out God's hand at His house of worship. His church is there for you. Great respect is given to the blind man or woman using a cane to venture out into the world alone, to the person that refuses being restricted by a wheelchair, and to a cancer victim and their caretaker. There are many tough challenges that people deal with today. The woman with the bent back is a perfect role model. Nothing kept her from worshipping her Lord.

Never forget the One that is right beside you, that loves you, and will be with you in your difficulties. Jesus has a hand in your life no matter the circumstance.

What comforts you most as you worship in the house of the Lord?

PRAYER

Lord, thank you for the cross. I reflect on how small my physical challenges are in comparison to your sacrifice. You make me feel valued whether I am in a time of peace or a period of challenge. I know you walk with me no matter my circumstance.

I appreciate my family and each person in my life. I know each individual is a unique blessing from you. May I see each one in the light of your love.

Thank you for the pleasure of getting up each morning and greeting the day with your joy in my heart. I know it is a gift from you. In Jesus' name, amen.

TODAY'S TRUTH

GOD IS BY YOUR SIDE NO MATTER THE CIRCUMSTANCE.

Jesus Heals a Man with Dropsy on the Sabbath

The Miracle of Truth

LUKE 14:1–6

Now it happened, as He went into the house of one of the rulers of the Pharisees to eat bread on the Sabbath, that they watched Him closely. And behold, there was a certain man before Him who had dropsy. And Jesus, answering, spoke to the lawyers and Pharisees, saying, "Is it lawful to heal on the Sabbath?"

But they kept silent. And He took him and healed him, and let him go. Then He answered them, saying, "Which of you, having a donkey or an ox that has fallen into a pit, will not immediately pull him out on the Sabbath day?" And they could not answer Him regarding these things.

GOING DEEPER

Jesus had been invited to one of the houses of a high-ranking Pharisee. The social status of the Pharisee ruler afforded opulent displays of meat, drink, and, if desired, entertainment when rulers hosted meals for people they felt were of a higher echelon of influence. Perhaps this dinner was one of those type meals. One thing we do know for sure, the Pharisees attending that dinner were hoping to trap Jesus into healing on the Sabbath or accuse Him falsely of an act of blasphemy.

They may not have understood Jesus fully, but He understood them well. Jesus knew the evil intent living in their hearts. As He entered the house, some lower class Jews lined the outer perimeters of the merriment. (Attendance of onlookers was an acceptable practice at occasions of the privileged.) A particular man watching stood out among the others, a man with dropsy. In Jesus' love and mercy, Jesus healed this man of his affliction. The man neither asked for healing nor offered thanks for the blessing he had just received. He was there, he was healed, he was gone.

Watching eyes, full of hostility and aloofness towards Jesus, were a sure indicator of their hatred for Him. So why was Jesus there? He was there because He had received a personal invitation. He did not go there for over indulgence and enjoyment, but to do good. This setting gave Him an opportunity to teach on many subjects. Perhaps He taught of mercy, of grace, of hypocrisy and false pretenses. We don't know all that He said, but the weapon He used to dismantle His foe was His truth—for God is truth.

PERSONAL REFLECTION

It is your decision where you go, what you do, and how you act and react in all situations. You are in control in the workplace, at home, at church, or out with friends having a good time. When you are in the company of groups of people, habits of self-indulgence may become apparent to you. Don't let suspect lifestyles sweep you off your feet. God will bring to mind His Scripture or perhaps other Biblical references to help you disarm the temptation. You can always choose to walk out of the toxic environment. You have the knowledge of God's will for your life; namely, to walk in a manner worthy of the Lord. Walk daily in the light of God's truth. When you walk with Him, you are in good company.

How is God's truth revealed in your walk with Him?

PRAYER

You are the truth, Father. I desire to walk in your ways. Help me to grow in your knowledge through the reading of your Word. I desire to be pleasing to you and do all things in my life according to your will. Help me bear fruit that encourages others to want to walk with you. Strengthen me when temptation crosses my path and allow me to be ever mindful that the Holy Spirit resides in me; that He is my guide and my friend. When I lay down at night to sleep, I want to have walked the day in a manner that pleases you. In His precious name I pray, amen.

TODAY'S TRUTH

GOD IS TRUTH.

DAY 35

Jesus Cleanses Ten Lepers
The Miracle of Thankfulness

LUKE 17:11–19

Now it happened as He went to Jerusalem that He passed through the midst of Samaria and Galilee. Then as He entered a certain village, there met Him ten men who were lepers, who stood afar off. And they lifted up their voices and said, "Jesus, Master, have mercy on us!"

So when He saw them, He said to them, "Go, show yourselves to the priests." And so it was that as they went, they were cleansed.

And one of them, when he saw that he was healed, returned, and with a loud voice glorified God, and fell down on his face at His feet, giving Him thanks. And he was a Samaritan.

So Jesus answered and said, "Were there not ten cleansed? But where *are* the nine? Were there not any found who returned to give glory to God except this foreigner?" And He said to him, "Arise, go your way. Your faith has made you well."

GOING DEEPER

The lepers begged for pity, not healing. They were probably asking Jesus for clothing, food, shelter, or whatever He could give them. That was the customary practice. That's what the *untouchables* did; they hung out in groups and begged for mercy, not healing.

Perhaps that is why the Samaritan was the only one who returned to give Jesus thanks after his healing. He understood the miracle that just happened. He knew he was an outcast, socially unfit, physically unclean, ritually unclean. He didn't expect anything but received more than he could ever have hoped. He received cleansing as he was following Jesus' command to see the priests. And he was grateful to the One that had cleansed him. He returned to thank Jesus. In doing so, he received a second life-changing gift. The leper was not only physically but spiritually healed. Among the ten former lepers, only the Samaritan hears the comforting words, "Your faith has made you well." His humble gratitude had revealed his belief. Jesus commends him for his response, for this man understood what had just happened to him, and Jesus appreciated it.

PERSONAL REFLECTION

Sometimes you just get busy with life—busy with work, busy with your family, busy with friends, just busy, busy, busy. How *can* you avoid your life becoming so full of activity that you don't have time to direct your heart to the things of the Lord?

Nine of the ten healed lepers were preoccupied with going to see the priests so they could be declared clean. They did not think to take the time to thank Jesus for His gift of healing. Now Jesus did tell them to go to the priests to be pronounced clean; however, shouldn't they have taken a minute to thank the One that was so kind and merciful to them? Perhaps they were anxious to become socially acceptable again.

Please don't let yourself become so busy that you ignore God's graciousness in your life. Take time to thank Him. Go to the throne with sincere gratitude in your heart. I think God will be glad to hear from you just as He was with the Samaritan.

In what ways do you show your thankfulness to the Lord?

PRAYER

Lord, you deserve all gratitude. You bestow grace and mercy freely. I thank you. There is such reassurance in knowing that I have a High Priest that cares about every detail of my life. I do not want busyness to overtake me. Would you reveal to me where my priorities are not in alignment with your will for my life? I want to; I need to hear your still, small voice.

I come to you with an appreciative heart for all your blessings in my life. Please forgive me when I forget to be mindful of your graciousness throughout the day. Thank you, Lord, for your faithfulness. My affection and appreciation I leave at your feet. Amen.

TODAY'S TRUTH

DON'T OVERLOOK
JESUS' GRACIOUSNESS
IN YOUR LIFE.

One Leper's Thanks*

By C. K Sharpe

Men, living flesh and spirit,
Lepers ten begging for healing,
Heart ready,
For grace and mercy.

Jesus, Lord, and King,
By spoken words
Healed and
Restored.

Praise and giving thanks
forgotten,
With back turned,
leaving and healed.

Was one thankful?

* Note: Read forward, poem tells of lepers encounter with Jesus.
   Read backward, the poem tells of just one leper's thankful heart.

DAY 36

Jesus Restores Sight to Bartimaeus

The Miracle of Mercy

MARK 10:46–52

Now they came to Jericho. As He went out of Jericho with His disciples and a great multitude, blind Bartimaeus, the son of Timaeus, sat by the road begging. And when he heard that it was Jesus of Nazareth, he began to cry out and say, "Jesus, Son of David, have mercy on me!"

Then many warned him to be quiet; but he cried out all the more, "Son of David, have mercy on me!"

So Jesus stood still and commanded him to be called.

Then they called the blind man, saying to him, "Be of good cheer. Rise, He is calling you."

And throwing aside his garment, he rose and came to Jesus.

So Jesus answered and said to him, "What do you want Me to do for you?"

The blind man said to Him, "Rabboni, that I may receive my sight."

Then Jesus said to him, "Go your way; your faith has made you well." And immediately he received his sight and followed Jesus on the road.

GOING DEEPER

On this day, as Bartimaeus begged for alms, he overheard news that Jesus, healer of sickness and forgiver of sins, would soon pass by the roadside where he sat. If Bartimaeus listened carefully, he could hear the shuffle from the untanned leather sandals worn by those in the crowd. He could even smell the dust in the air stirred up by all the shuffling feet. Soon he heard the clamor of the crowds coming, as well as chatter from others lining the roadside. Bartimaeus wondered how he was going to get Jesus' attention with all that commotion.

Bartimaeus waited. He listened. He knew, *he believed*, what he had heard about Jesus. Bartimaeus was blind, and desperately wanted to be healed. So as he heard Jesus approaching, he persistently cried out—louder and louder—to the One that could save him from his wretched condition.

Jesus heard him cry out for mercy. Jesus called for him. In his disadvantaged state, Bartimaeus went to *Jesus* to beg for healing. Jesus respected his determination and saw the belief that Bartimaeus displayed. In His mercy, Jesus granted Bartimaeus' request.

Jesus can take a lost person who is spiritually blind to his condition (blind to his sin and blind to his doomed eternity) and through His mercy, Jesus forgives and provides a new life in Him. That is what happened to Bartimaeus.

After healing and salvation, Bartimaeus' direction in life was changed forever. He had thrown off his cloak of burden and instead of going his way, he followed Jesus and glorified God. A new life for him had begun.

PERSONAL REFLECTION

There may be a desire you have today that only Jesus can fulfill.
Let your heart call out to Him. Your faith can be as bold as Bartimaeus, the kind of faith that pleases God. He had complete trust
in his Savior. Delight the Lord as Bartimaeus did. If you have a
cloak of sin—guilt, rebellion, lack of forgiveness, or whatever it
may be—throw it off and call out for Jesus' mercy.

Jesus was on a *path* that led to the cross. There He would give
His soul for all. Bartimaeus was on a *path* that found Jesus, result-
ing in healing and a changed soul. You too can stop Jesus right
in the middle of your path. Call out to the merciful One. There
may be some people in your life that tell you to be quiet (as some
told Bartimaeus), but there are other friends and encouragers
that tell you that He is calling for you.

What stained cloak do you need
to exchange for God's mercy?

PRAYER

*Jesus, thank you for your voice in my life. Help me to become
a Bartimaeus-type believer. A want to be a person that will
never leave you but will always remember that first touch of
rebirth I experienced through you. I want to be one that follows you and proclaims the power of your name boldly.*

*Every word in the Bible is your voice. As I read the Scrip-
tures, I desire to hear your voice clearly and have a responsive
heart that develops my character. Through your mercy, I*

desire to be a person that can be used by you. The only cloak I need is to be cloaked in your Word.

Thank you, Father, for I know you will give me everything I need to serve you. Help me to use your gifts wisely. Amen.

TODAY'S TRUTH

JESUS IS MERCIFUL.

Jesus Heals a Servant's Severed Ear
The Miracle of Control Over Evil

JOHN 18:1–12; LUKE 22:51

When Jesus had spoken these words, He went out with His disciples over the Brook Kidron, where there was a garden, which He and His disciples entered. And Judas, who betrayed Him, also knew the place; for Jesus often met there with His disciples. Then Judas, having received a detachment of troops, and officers from the chief priests and Pharisees, came there with lanterns, torches, and weapons. Jesus therefore, knowing all things that would come upon Him, went forward and said to them, "Whom are you seeking?"

They answered Him, "Jesus of Nazareth."

Jesus said to them, "I am He." And Judas, who betrayed Him, also stood with them. Now when He said to them, "I am He," they drew back and fell to the ground.

Then He asked them again, "Whom are you seeking?"

And they said, "Jesus of Nazareth."

Jesus answered, "I have told you that I am He. Therefore, if you seek Me, let these go their way," that the saying might be fulfilled which He spoke, "Of those whom You gave Me I have lost none."

Then Simon Peter, having a sword, drew it and struck the high priest's servant, and cut off his right ear. The servant's name was Malchus.

So Jesus said to Peter, "Put your sword into the sheath. Shall I not drink the cup which My Father has given Me?"

Then the detachment of troops and the captain and the officers of the Jews arrested Jesus and bound Him.

•••

But Jesus answered and said, "Permit even this." And He touched his ear and healed him.

Going Deeper

Satan and his evil powers are alive and well. This hope for dominance was apparent by Judas' cohort (six hundred soldiers) that flanked the garden along with Jewish officers and probably others who wanted to see Jesus' demise. Little did they realize that it was Jesus who was in control, not them. Jesus held the power to accomplish His Father's purpose. By praying to His heavenly Father, the sinless, selfless, humble Jesus knew that His act of submission in the garden of Gethsemane would lead to the culmination of God's plan. Jesus would be the propitiation for humanity's sin. All glory and power were His. He was the face of God.

Jesus' death would be the beginning of the end of satan's power of seduction. Satan may have thought he had won the battle between good and evil in the Garden of Eden when he introduced sin to humanity, but he didn't. God cast Adam and Eve out of the Garden for their grievous actions, but the all-knowing God had a plan for human redemption. And it involved His only Son.

Nothing came as a surprise to the Lord. In fact, Jesus' death on the cross was satan's biggest defeat; the great deceiver had finally deceived himself. Evil may have caused Judas to betray the Master, caused the hasty severing of an ear, but there is certainly nothing that can stop the will of God.

Jesus' thoughts have never been and never will be about Himself, but directed toward those He loves: His bride, His church. God's will was being done. The days that followed proved that.

Personal Reflection

Jesus made His soul an offering. It was a free gift given to you. You need not fall back as the cohort did when Jesus spoke to the very essence of God, the ultimate reality, *I AM He.*

Jesus prayed to His Father that His will be done. You too, through prayer, have the freedom to go to King Jesus and speak with Him on whatever topic concerns you. No one will hold you captive as they tried to do with Jesus in the garden. You are His delight, and He looks forward to your time together.

Jesus was in complete control in the garden, and He is still in control. Nothing happens to you or any of His loved ones without the approval of God. He knows your name. He willingly went with His captors. He was the ultimate free-will offering.

*How do you use the free gift
Jesus has given you?*

Prayer

Father, my thoughts take me back to the garden when Jesus proclaimed who He was. I muse over the falling back of the dumbstruck as the veil of deceit was taken from their eyes in the garden as they recognized the great I AM, the holy One of God. How vast is your awesome power. Nothing is accomplished unless it is according to your will. I am so thankful, God, that you have a plan for my life, and that you love me so much that you call me by name. My heart is full as I recognize, as the cohorts in the garden did, how great thou art, Lord. Amen.

TODAY'S TRUTH

JESUS HAS COMPLETE CONTROL OVER EVERY SITUATION.

PART VI

RESURRECTION AND ASCENSION

The Preeminence
and Resurrection of Christ

The Miracle of Jesus' Supremacy

He is despised and rejected by men,
A Man of sorrows and acquainted with grief.
And we hid, as it were, our faces from Him;
He was despised, and we did not esteem Him.

Surely He has borne our griefs
And carried our sorrows;
Yet we esteemed Him stricken,
Smitten by God, and afflicted.
 But He was wounded for our transgressions,
He was bruised for our iniquities;
The chastisement for our peace was upon Him,
And by His stripes we are healed.
 All we like sheep have gone astray;
We have turned, every one, to his own way;
And the Lord has laid on Him the iniquity of us all.

He was oppressed and He was afflicted,
Yet He opened not His mouth;
He was led as a lamb to the slaughter,

And as a sheep before its shearers is silent,
So He opened not His mouth.

•••

After the Sabbath, at dawn on the first day of the week, Mary Magdalene and the other Mary went to look at the tomb.

There was a violent earthquake, for an angel of the Lord came down from heaven and, going to the tomb, rolled back the stone and sat on it. His appearance was like lightning, and his clothes were white as snow. The guards were so afraid of him that they shook and became like dead men.

The angel said to the women, "Do not be afraid, for I know that you are looking for Jesus, who was crucified. He is not here; he has risen, just as he said. Come and see the place where he lay. Then go quickly and tell his disciples: 'He has risen from the dead and is going ahead of you into Galilee. There you will see him.' Now I have told you."

So the women hurried away from the tomb, afraid yet filled with joy, and ran to tell his disciples. Suddenly Jesus met them. "Greetings," he said. They came to him, clasped his feet and worshiped him. Then Jesus said to them, "Do not be afraid. Go and tell my brothers to go to Galilee; there they will see me."

GOING DEEPER

Jesus was born with a purpose. That purpose was to be the world's sin-bearer; the One that was sent to complete the Father's plan of salvation. Jesus was the only one that could satisfy that purpose. He is the Creator and the supreme Being; meaning Jesus is God. In Colossians 2:9 it states clearly, "For in Christ all the fullness of the Deity lives in bodily form" (NIV).

Let's take a moment to reflect on His death. Before Jesus was led to the cross, one could hear the weeping of Jesus' followers as brutalities were inflicted on Him. They tortured Him to the point of being unrecognizable. We do not dare reflect on the indecencies that He later sustained at Calvary for our pained hearts would be overcome by the burden for the One who bore our sins.

Through His holy eyes, we were worth the price He paid to redeem us. He paid it all at Calvary. Jesus was the sinless blood sacrifice; the perfect ransom for our souls. No matter our race, religion, background, or the magnitude or number of our sins, He knew, and knows today, nothing but everlasting love for us. Hanging there on the cross, Jesus absorbed our sins into Himself. He became our sin. Jesus did this to keep us from eternal separation from God.

As we continue our reflection, let's parallel Abraham's anguish when he was told to offer his son as a sacrifice in the region of Moriah. God saw Abraham's faithfulness and supplied a ram as an alternate burnt offering. As the years passed, God looked upon an unworthy world that also was in need of atonement. He did for us as He did for Abraham. God supplied the ultimate sin sacrifice for the world—His son.

PERSONAL REFLECTION

God's love for you lasts an eternity. You are His chosen and are being built-up as part of His spiritual house. Scripture tells you that Jesus was not despised and rejected because of any flaw in Himself. He never sinned nor talked ill of anyone. Those that despised Him did not see the beauty of His holiness. They rejected His word and His work. Little did they recognize that

Jesus was the cornerstone on which the church was being built. You are to align yourself with the Chief Cornerstone which enables His church to be straight and true. Remember, God does not look at one's outward appearance, but looks at the heart. He does not shun or reject. You belong to Jesus.

How does God reign in your heart?

PRAYER

Father, your supremacy is displayed in all your works. You are a mighty and giving God. Thank you, Father, for your sacrificial offering of your beloved Son. I pray in gratitude knowing you place so much love and value on the human soul that you sent your Son to earth as a baby to a life of poverty, rejection, suffering, and ultimately death. All of this He gladly did so He could seek and save lost souls. Jesus took the pain of the cross so that we might receive new life through Him. I learned from Colossians 1:18 that Jesus is the head of the body, the church: who is the beginning, the firstborn from the dead; that in all things he might have the preeminence.

I humble myself before you. May my life be found strong as you build up your Church. Thank you for your atoning grace. I say this in the name of our Lord and Savior, amen.

TODAY'S TRUTH

OUR SUPREME GOD LOVES AND DELIGHTS IN US EVEN UNTO DEATH.

Blood-Washed Cross

By C. K. Sharpe

Scepters scourge to gratify shameless souls,
Crowds scorn and laugh as ancient scrolls foretold.
Soldier nails set Deliverer to Calvary's tree,
Others cast lots for His garment upon bended knee.

Rough-hewn placard placed above thorn-crowned head,
"This Is Jesus the King of the Jews" it said.
As wrath poured out on Messiah, Glory turned away,
Scarlet drops of blood bought sinners, dross that day.

Fulfillment of Scriptures was completed by God's plan,
Buying souls deliverance through sacrificial lamb.
Jesus is sin's propitiation in humanity's stead,
Heaven's firstborn, ALIVE, risen from the dead!

Ascension of Jesus

The Miracle of Rising to Heaven

ACTS 1:1–11

The former account I made, O Theophilus, of all that Jesus began both to do and teach, until the day in which He was taken up, after He through the Holy Spirit had given commandments to the apostles whom He had chosen, to whom He also presented Himself alive after His suffering by many infallible proofs, being seen by them during forty days and speaking of the things pertaining to the kingdom of God.

And being assembled together with them, He commanded them not to depart from Jerusalem, but to wait for the Promise of the Father, "which," He said, "you have heard from Me; for John truly baptized with water, but you shall be baptized with the Holy Spirit not many days from now." Therefore, when they had come together, they asked Him, saying, "Lord, will You at this time restore the kingdom to Israel?" And He said to them, "It is not for you to know times or seasons which the Father has put in His own authority. But you shall receive power when the Holy Spirit has come upon you; and you shall be witnesses to Me in Jerusalem, and in all Judea and Samaria, and to the end of the earth."

Now when He had spoken these things, while they watched, He was taken up, and a cloud received Him out of their sight.

And while they looked steadfastly toward heaven as He went up, behold, two men stood by them in white apparel, who also said, "Men of Galilee, why do you stand gazing up into heaven? This same Jesus, who was taken up from you into heaven, will so come in like manner as you saw Him go into heaven."

GOING DEEPER

Jesus going home: Jesus ascended into heaven to prepare a place for His own and be about His Father's business. He left the apostles with words of instruction, hope, and joy. He told them that He was ascending *unto My Father and your Father, and to My God, and your God.* He had just completed forty days among the people, preaching and healing and showing them that through God's power He had been resurrected. He was eternally alive.

What a beautiful sight it must have been to witness God taking up His Son; watching Jesus leave this world surrounded by God's glory in the form of a cloud. And, once home, how majestic it must have been to be seated in His rightful place at His Father's right hand.

Spirit's new home: Jesus told His disciples they were not losing Him, but He would be with them in a different way, through His Spirit. And it wouldn't be long before the Holy Spirit would come upon them. The Holy Spirit's home is in the heart of each believer. Having been given this knowledge, it is the responsibility of each believer to exercise the faith of the Spirit; to believe the Word, live and pray in the Word, and listen to the Spirit. God is then able to work powerfully through His believers.

Believer's eternal home: We are to be patient for the return of the Lord as He is patient. It is believed that Jesus is waiting for

His *fruit of the earth* to ripen. That would be His chosen. In the meantime, we are to continue to grow in righteousness, wrestle against the ruler of the darkness of this world, be strong in our suffering, and remain obedient to His Word. We are to read our Bible and pray, asking the Spirit to show us the truth and teach us how to live. As believers, we are excited for the Lord's harvest and going to our eternal home. Until the appointed time, we must be about our Father's business.

PERSONAL REFLECTION

You also can be about your Father's business. You can help in the restoration of His family. You may not think you are ready for such a responsibility, but you, with every other believer, are growing in faith and learning His Word. You are ready. He can use you right where you are today. You can count it as a joy to love and serve Him while you are on earth. You have been charged to share the good news of salvation.

It is not always easy to share the Word with others. Those nasty demons are running around trying to disrupt your good work. Persevere. There is no greater pleasure than telling others about Jesus and planting the seed of salvation in their hearts. Tell them how Jesus can release the pains of their heart. If you feel led, give them your testimony. People like to know that they are not alone in their earthly struggles.

Tell of the never-ending blessedness of an eternity that awaits them in heaven. A place where they may call home, too, if they so desire. Dear one, His purpose for your life will prevail as you give Him the glory and He continues to reap His soul harvest. How precious you are to Him!

---

*What are you doing when you
are about God's business?*

PRAYER

I am grateful to you, Jesus, for your ascension and the Holy
Spirit you sent, which guides me into the truths of the gospel.
Give me boldness and freedom to confess your truths before
others. I know there will be times when your Word is beyond
their discernment. At these times give me boldness through
you to clarify your Spirit of truth. Help me to hide your Word
in my heart so when I need it, it will come forth as a redemptive opportunity for collegues, friends, and family.

Thank you for the regeneration of souls and spiritual con-
version. My prayer is that the Holy Spirit becomes a close
friend to many I know. He dwells in me and for this understanding of truth, I glorify your name. Amen.

TODAY'S TRUTH

JESUS LIVES
AND THE HOLY SPIRIT
RESIDES IN US.

Part VII

NEW BIRTH
IN CHRIST

The Ministry of Reconciliation
The Miracle of New Birth in Christ

2 CORINTHIANS 5:10–21 NASB

For we must all appear before the judgment seat of Christ, so that each one may be recompensed for his deeds in the body, according to what he has done, whether good or bad.

Therefore, knowing the fear of the Lord, we persuade men, but we are made manifest to God; and I hope that we are made manifest also in your consciences. We are not again commending ourselves to you but are giving you an occasion to be proud of us, so that you will have an answer for those who take pride in appearance and not in heart. For if we are beside ourselves, it is for God; if we are of sound mind, it is for you. For the love of Christ controls us, having concluded this, that one died for all, therefore all died; and He died for all, so that they who live might no longer) live for themselves, but for Him who died and rose again on their behalf.

Therefore from now on we recognize no one according to the flesh; even though we have known Christ according to the flesh, yet now we know Him in this way no longer. Therefore if anyone is in Christ, he is a new creature; the old things passed away; behold, new things have come. Now all these things are from God, who reconciled us to Himself through Christ and gave us the ministry of reconciliation, namely, that God was in

Christ reconciling the world to Himself, not counting their trespasses against them, and He has committed to us the word of reconciliation.

Therefore, we are ambassadors for Christ, as though God were making an appeal through us; we beg you on behalf of Christ, be reconciled to God. He made Him who knew no sin to be sin on our behalf, so that we might become the righteousness of God in Him.

GOING DEEPER

Believe. This powerful word is often used in the Bible. Belief is the crux of Biblical faith. It leads to reconciliation with God, assurance of salvation through Jesus Christ, and the leading of the Holy Spirit in our life. We believe we have been given a new life through the death, burial, and resurrection of Jesus Christ. We trust, have faith, and are confident that God's Word is true; that we have been born again through His completed work on the cross.

B = Believe what the Bible teaches about Jesus Christ (John 3:16).

E = Entirely rest in the character and promises of God (Joshua 23:14).

L = Love others with Godly love. Share the good news of Christ (Mark 16:15–16).

I = Imparts new spiritual life in us; used in the context of being born again (John 3:3–8).

E = Enter into fellowship and hearing the Word with other Christians (1 John 1:3).

V = Value the messages and saving Word of Jesus (John 5:24).

E = Enjoy learning and growing in the sanctification of the Lord (2 Timothy 2:21).

We have been tasked by God to reconcile people to Him. Since we believe that the Bible is the only standard of truth and Jesus is the only way to salvation, we are ready to answer God's call. What a privilege it is to be God's ambassador.

PERSONAL REFLECTION

If you do not have the hope of Jesus Christ in your life, it is not too late to give your life to Him. You can do it right now. His arms are outstretched waiting for you to come to Him. What matters to Him is what is inside your heart. Be honest with Him. Pour your heart out to Him. He loves you, and He is a compassionate listener. He wants a personal relationship with you.

Why not start your new life in Christ right now. Confess to Him that you are a sinner (Romans 3:10), and you are willing to turn from your sin (Acts 17:30). Confess that you believe that Jesus Christ died for you, was buried and rose again from the dead, and that He paid the price for your sins (Romans 10:9–10). If you agree with these questions, all that is left for you to do is pray and invite Jesus into your heart as your Lord and Savior (Romans 10:13).

God's saving grace can be yours by praying these simple, life-changing words below:

Jesus, I know I am a sinner. I ask you to forgive me all my sins. Right now, I repent and turn from sinning and doing wrong. I believe you died to pay for my sins and rose from the dead. I ask you to seal me in your precious blood. Please come into my heart, right now as my Lord and Savior. Fill me with your Holy Spirit. I will trust and follow you. Direct my life and help me to do your will. In your precious name Jesus, I pray for eternal salvation. Amen.

If you just prayed to the Lord for your salvation, you probably want to shout it from the rooftop. Luke 15:10 tells us that angels are rejoicing over you in heaven right now. Isn't that great! You caused joy in heaven!

There is no better way to honor the joy of your salvation than by going to His house of worship. Why not call a Christian friend and tell them of your decision? May God's blessing be with you as you begin or continue your journey with Jesus. Oh, what a friend we have in Jesus.

What opportunities have you had to be God's ambassador?

PRAYER

Oh Lord, mighty to save, your love controls me, and I wouldn't have it any other way. You have put before me the truth, and I delight in it. Your Scripture tells me that I am a new creation, old things have passed away, and all things have become new. I have been reconciled through the blood of Jesus Christ. You have given me the ministry of reconciliation. Thank you, God, for the privilege of being your child.

According to Psalm 96:2–3, we are to "Sing to the LORD; praise his name. Each day proclaim the good news that he saves. Publish his glorious deeds among the nations. Tell everyone about the amazing things he does" (NLT).

May the Holy Spirit fill my heart with so much gladness that my passion tumbles forth "to all that have ears to hear" of your everlasting love. In the saving name of Jesus, amen.

SPECIAL THANKS

To Mary L., Trudy P., Evelyn G., and Lori S., for their unfailing support and true friendship (Proverbs 27:17).

To Carol D., my twin sister, for her great encouragement and passionate love of the Lord (Ecclesiastes 4:9).

To my dear husband, Tom. He is a great partner and leader in my life. By his love and support, he helped me enjoy every minute of my quest. (It made for some great spiritual discussions too.)

I have a deep faith in God and acknowledge Jesus Christ as my Lord and Savior. May His will be accomplished through these writings. With praise, I dedicate this devotional to God; the Creator of all things and who in His infinite wisdom has given me the desire to serve Him in this way.

About the Author

Cheryl enjoys a big cup of hot coffee, a roaring fire, and a great inspirational book. She has brought her love of the written word to many aspects of her life: from school and local newspapers to writing devotionals and a Bible study.

She currently resides in Georgia with her husband, Tom. She has two grown children, is the proud grandmother of seven, and is the owner of a loving Keeshond that is always at her side.

Her gift of faith has enabled her to be an encourager and doer of the Word. She spent many years as a Sunday school teacher, an advocate in children and teen grief ministries, and a participant in community outreach projects that encouraged others to put their trust and hope in Jesus, no matter their current circumstance. As a volunteer for several worthy organizations during her life, she has shared biblical principles through Bible studies for mothers and written vignettes for children. This support helped them to connect, build character, and make a difference in their community and schools.

She has found that joy through Jesus Christ really does begin in the heart. Through Him, she is living an abundant and satisfying life.

For more on Cheryl, go to her website:
myfaithkeys.com
or to Facebook, Author_C.K. Sharpe